THE MONK MIND

A spiritual and holistic life illuminated

Mytri SanatKumar

Copyright © Mytri SanatKumar
All Rights Reserved.

This book has been self-published with all reasonable efforts taken to make the material error-free by the author. No part of this book shall be used, reproduced in any manner whatsoever without written permission from the author, except in the case of brief quotations embodied in critical articles and reviews.

The Author of this book is solely responsible and liable for its content including but not limited to the views, representations, descriptions, statements, information, opinions and references ["Content"]. The Content of this book shall not constitute or be construed or deemed to reflect the opinion or expression of the Publisher or Editor. Neither the Publisher nor Editor endorse or approve the Content of this book or guarantee the reliability, accuracy or completeness of the Content published herein and do not make any representations or warranties of any kind, express or implied, including but not limited to the implied warranties of merchantability, fitness for a particular purpose. The Publisher and Editor shall not be liable whatsoever for any errors, omissions, whether such errors or omissions result from negligence, accident, or any other cause or claims for loss or damages of any kind, including without limitation, indirect or consequential loss or damage arising out of use, inability to use, or about the reliability, accuracy or sufficiency of the information contained in this book.

Made with ❤ on the Notion Press Platform
www.notionpress.com

Gratitude

My prayer and gratitude to all the beings of the lower and higher realms of existence.

My prayer and gratitude to all my teachers of the past, present, and future.

My sincere gratitude to all the monks of Bharat (India) and Sri Lanka for their love, patience, and kindness toward me.

To my parents, who have accepted me as I am and nurtured me with virtues and boundless affection.

My gratitude will be incomplete without the mention of my master and friend, Sri Tathata, who is solely responsible for guiding me on the path of purification.

Contents

Contents

Introduction

In this day and age, we have the probable answers to most of our problems, yet the everlasting search for some kind of peace and contentment has not yet ceased. All the ancestors of the human race even thought it was necessary to find or go in search of that sort of contentment, but in recent times, the human race has not found it important enough to even attempt to try for that kind of search. Since the search for that inner contentment never ends, one might abide by the logic that if the quest for so many generations has not yet ended, one might as well move in the direction that is more apparent.

Sometimes one might think to take refuge in religion or follow some dos and don'ts. But the cardinal question lies in one's meditation on the question of arriving at that state of contentment or simplicity. Coming to a state of mind that is emancipated from a conundrum of thoughts. What one feels is a feeling in the gut that says, What next? Where am I going? And what is the purpose?

One has to see that one's own actions and thought processes have divided their lives into sections of success and failure based on the parameters of money, fame, power, and social influence. Even being termed successful by the standards of society, this internal quest, which leads one to a perpetual state of calm and contentment, remains unresolved. It is some sort of hunger; the hungrier one gets, one tries to consume more to satisfy the hunger, then all that is eaten is again flushed out by the body, and this cycle keeps on repeating. Similar are one's actions in the physical and mental worlds. The physical realms are met, and in the due process, a mental consequence is created. That impression of the consequence remains in the mental sphere. Depending on the mental effect of that consequence, it leads to another set of physical actions on the basis of that emotion, and this cycle goes on and on. This cycle of mental and physical chain reactions leads to the question, 'What is enough?' Even though we achieve the goals of fame, power, success, and influence, there is a feeling of emptiness. This leads to a series of questions that one asks to quench that internal hunger or that feeling of emptiness: "Is it Yoga?" "Is it meditation?" "Is it prayer?" "Is it religion?" "Is it church?" "Is it a temple?" "Is it a guru?" These questions, even though quintessential, do not, in their individual aspects, satiate the underlying emotion of unfulfillment. Not denying the importance of their individualistic importance in one's life, the effort here is to develop an understanding of the mind in the question that makes one think in the directions of these questions and to develop a basis where one can treat oneself by having a proper understanding and perspective while answering the aforementioned questions.

Does success defined by material parameters like fame, money, power, and influence, or is success defined by spiritual parameters like emancipation or psychic powers, lead us to solving this mystery of the internal quest? The understanding here is to be free from any goal setting or labeling and to be as natural as possible. The habit of setting goals in the material world, e.g., relationship goals or financial goals, one tends to replicate that system of labeling and goal-setting in the spiritual world or the non-material world. Goals like self-realization, emancipation, and psychic powers often create a hindrance (because of the blind superimposition of such thoughts from books and teachings of spiritual masters) rather than a smooth pathway for one to be simpler and more effortless in understanding one's own mental and physical conditions. I am not denying the existence of such higher states of mind, but the question here is: does one really need to set up such goals, or is it to create such mental and physical conditions that lead to such higher states of understanding and a continued state of bliss and happiness naturally? The basis of the spiritual world is being totally goal-free. What is this goal—a free, simple, and natural state of mind?

The individual usually trains himself or herself to be successful in life by obtaining a proper knowledge base and training for doing so in their respective fields. Does one really gather information, knowledge, or training about one's way of being? What would be the knowledge base and training of habit patterns that make one achieve worldly parameters and higher internal states of being? What does it take for one to be successful in the world as well as develop into a higher state of mental and physical being? How does one go to a spiritual master and understand his philosophy to the fullest? How does one enter a religion and understand its practices deeply? How does one enter monkhood and understand the true essentials of that particular life? How does the individual find answers to questions about life on the inside rather than searching on the outside?

The answer lies in developing the "monk – mind". Monk-mind, not in the sense of leaving the world or its objects but building up a psyche of non-attachment and simplicity. In simple words, it is getting to a state of mind where the mind is getting more transparent with its own objects and the objects it cognizes from the material sphere. This transparent mind state, or the Monk – Mind is a state of mind without any labels or goals. The monk-mind can cognize any particular situation in its entirety and understand it without any emotions describing that situation that arise in the faculties of the mind; rather, it is to observe the situation "as it is." The Monk – Mind is a state where it helps one to confront and recognize one's own self-affirmations, like an actor who takes on different roles as the script requires the actor to be in. Similarly, the Monk – Mind is a state of cognition where one understands the roles one has to undertake in daily life with utmost perfection, but deep down, one should be aware that these roles in their entirety do not exemplify existence vis-à-vis an actor. For instance, one is a doctor in a hospital while treating patients; the doctor is a physician while instructing a junior doctor; he is a teacher; and at the same time, at home, the doctor is a father to his child; a son to parents; a husband to a wife; a citizen of a country;

and so, on and so forth. The monk- mind is a state of awareness where the person in the above condition realizes his disassociation with these aforementioned roles in their singular existence. The overlapping of these spheres of existence creates confusion, anxiety, and sorrow in the mental space. Most importantly, the monk-mind is a state of evolution where one can observe in true existence that the acceptance of these spheres of existence as permanent is a fallacy, and wisdom lies in the temporal nature of these roles or the spheres of existence. When these spheres of self-existence succumb due to their non-permanency, it leads to neurosis, which further leads to sorrow, anxiety, and fear.

To be free from the fear, sorrow, and delusion that manifest in creation, this book acts as a pathfinder to allow one to be better equipped to handle these complexities of emotion that occur both in the external and spiritual aspects of one's existence. This acts as a stable ground for developing a simple state of mind for the acceptance of the nature of the constantly evolving nature of creation.

Factors of the Monk – Mind

To understand the monk-mind, it is important to understand the features of the mind one is going to work on to attain the state of the monk-mind. These are terms related to different states of the mind and the root cause of an individual's being. These terms are to be frequented in the flow of the book and need to be understood in a proper context.

Karmic Conditionings

Every individual or being in the universe is unique and diverse in their own way of being. The reason for that is the presence of a unique karmic conditioning behind the individual. When an individual goes to shop for a record in a music shop, the record of a particular genre is written on the record disc. Similarly, the individual comes into the universe with pre-set conditions of mental and physical factors based on their karmic conditions. Just like in a record shop, different genres of music have a particular style of music depending on the artist's writing on the record.

The individual's own karmic conditions have been delivered into the creation in accordance with the genre of past actions and their impressions of mental and physical factors. These factors unfold with the movement of time and change in space. The change of space and the movement of time depend upon the karmic conditions. The mental factors result in a particular mental state and self-affirmations of the individual, and the physical factors result in the region, community, physical body, family, and surroundings of the individual. One has come into existence to experience the karmic conditionings of one, just like a record label has been bought to listen to a particular type of music. The particular type of music that is the result of the impression on the record signifies the physical and mental factors of the individual and, most importantly, the self-affirmations of the individual.

Self-Affirmations

The impressions of the karmic conditionings have resulted in the self-affirmations of the individual. As the record is played on the player, with each rotation of the disc, there arises a different note of music at a particular time period, which gives rise to the melody of the song. The song as a whole signifies the life of the individual in creation. The entirety of the song is created by the different pitches and notes that arise at different and selected time periods. Each note and pitch that arises at these fixed intervals depicts the different self-affirmations the individual has to go through. Each note has an effect on the music, which creates a certain effect on the listener's mind. This effect of the note is similar to the duties and actions one has to undertake during the time period of the self-affirmations. The self-affirmations come with a set of duties and actions that need to be carried out.

The Conditioned Mind

To continue the example of the music record, the conditioned mind can be compared to a faulty record player.

The fault in the record player can be identified by its inability to play the music written on the record. The reasons for the fault may be many, but one can usually see and hear the record being stuck and its inability to revolve freely. The natural law that governs existence is of continuous movement or change; the conditioned mind, just like the faulty record player, isn't able to understand, cognize, or be in synchronization with the natural flow and law of life, which is of constant movement and change.

When one usually listens to a broken record player, it usually gets stuck on a note on the record and keeps on playing. The conditioned mind, which goes against the natural flow of life, gets affirmed into the delusion of permanence and gets attached to the self—affirmation—and to the duties related to it. This sense of permanence makes the individual think that self-affirmations are everlasting. That is why the thought of permanence is one of confusion rather than clarity. When one individual listens to the broken record player, it becomes unbearable after a point of time and creates a feeling of uneasiness and pain in one's being. This feeling of pain is equivalent to the emotions that arise from the delusion of permanence, which are anger, jealousy, hatred, etcetera, or, in short, an unwholesome state of being or mind that has arisen from the habit of expectation. These emotions and actions again become a reason for the impressions of new karmic conditionings. As the karmic conditionings of this life are not experienced and understood, a new set of conditions gets written in the mental realm. A broken record player does not play the music written on the record properly but also becomes a cause for the destruction of the record by distorting the written music on it, just like the conditioned mind. The root causes of the conditioned mind are the habit patterns of the individual and the effects of the society, culture, and region in which one lives. It is not that these factors in themselves have a fault, but the view of permanence is such that the individual confirms one's totality in existence as being confirmed or described by these factors. This is because, the nature of the mind is to hold onto some object or a conditioning for affirming one's own ease of existence. But the true nature of constant change which is natural to the creation always takes over this artificial sense of being that is of permanence. When this natural law of change and evolution takes place, it gives rise to anxiety and fear which acts as a basis for the creation of other defilements in one's own way of being. For evolution to take place there needs to be constant creation and destruction. With the destruction of existing self – affirmations and the birth of a new self – affirmations at a given point of time, it creates an environment or space for generating anxiety and fear due to the presence of the conditioned mind which does not allow the individual to understand and view the natural law of impermanence and evolution. The presence of the conditioned mind is based on the ease which it gives the individual by affirming to permanence of the self – affirmations.

The Monk-Mind

The monk - mind is the state of mind that is in synchronization with the law of existence, which is the natural flow of life, impermanence, and change. Impermanence of the self-affirmations and the duties or actions associated with them the natural or the monk – mind state is similar to the record player, which is devoid of any faults. The fault here is the presence of the conditioned mind. The music on the record gets played perfectly, and the music ends. With the development of the monk – mind the individual is able to complete and understand the self-affirmations that arise as time passes by and change accordingly without getting stuck or confirmed at a particular stage of life. One is able to change and adapt accordingly. The individual is able to glide with the flow of life without being stuck. The question that arises is what comes next after the music ends or the impressions of the self-affirmations are exhausted in their experience and understanding. The monk-mind not only ensures that the karmic conditions are played out completely, but new conditions also do not get written on in the mental realm. The conditions of the self are exhausted, and there begins the divine life, or life based on synchronization with the whole of existence, where existence and the individual become one. Nature starts to play its role through the individual. With this base, the individual starts climbing higher and developing more refined mental states.

To develop a monk-mind, it is very important to develop the correct intention behind it. The intention of the monk - mind is to get simpler in life. To be basic and simpler in life is to understand the complexity of the illusion that is presented in front of one. This understanding is then the vital ingredient for the equanimity of acceptance that arises, which helps one to be free from the sorrow and fear that are the resultants of the illusion that arises. What is the illusion? It is the thought of the permanency of the self-affirmations. This simplicity and the basic natural mind, now referred to as the monk-mind, develop immunity to this illusion. It is like the strength and elasticity of a rubber band. The higher the strength of elasticity, the greater the strength of stretch the rubber band can experience. Similarly, the stretch here is sorrow, grief, and many complex emotions that arise in one due to the illusion of permanence in the self-affirmations; the strength of elasticity is the depth of the monk-mind developed by one. The higher the strength of one's mind, one is able to adapt and understand the impermanent nature of the emotions that arise in life, which leads one to be free from them. Monk – Mind is to have that natural and basic state of mind. When a piano maestro is teaching the pupil, the mentor always focuses on getting the basics right by making the pupil practice the basic notes with a lot of repetitions slowly and steadily for a long period of time, and in due course, the complex notes can be played with utmost ease, just like muscle memory. The Monk - Mind slowly yet steadily readies the mind to be free from the attachment of self-affirmations by developing a strong immunity structure through the process of practice and insight, factors of the monk lifestyle. The monk-mind trains one to be slowly and steadily free from these affirmations and their effects through practice and insight, leading the mind to be simple and basic in nature, through which it acquires immunity from the neurosis of the passing away of these self-affirmations. The monk-mind, through its immunity, tries to dissect the complexities of emotion arising in the mind. In the world, practice is perceived as monks sitting cross-legged with closed eyes in caves and on mountain peaks. Is this the practice that is aimed at here? The effort here is to manifest the mental space of those solitude-stricken monks in the everyday mind. The mental space is the silence and beauty of those caves and beautiful mountain peaks. The Monk-Mind is a real-time replica of the silence of the cave and Himalayan monasteries in everyday life. This beautiful, simple, natural, and basic mental state is to be developed through practice, insights, and the factors of monk lifestyle. This state of mind is free from all the goal-setting and race that is endured by one in everyday life. There is no denouncing goal-setting or running the race in the world, yet it is to create a wholsome mental space. Even while doing these actions, one is settled and sees through the impermanence of these things by letting things unfold in their own ways without any labeling of the mind.

To understand the unfolding of things in the mental space, one must be aware of the knowledge of one's existence, i.e., that one's existence is the sum result of one's past actions. This awareness is the awareness of one's karmic conditions. The present is the unfolding of past karmic actions. The mind, due to one's affinity to the self-affirmations, is not attenuated to the karmic conditions. This distortion is the root cause of sorrow, anxiety, and delusion. This distorted mind, which is in frequency with self-affirmation, is the "conditioned mind." The monk-mind is the mind that is in total synchronization with the karmic conditions, i.e., when the mind is able to observe the unfolding of the past and present actions and, with a deeper practice, know the future conditionings of one's actions, or karma. This state of mind is trying to evolve. The monk-mind is a way of evolving to that immunity or strength of elasticity to comprehend the karmic enfoldments with a clear mental picture, just like a monk sitting in a cave or at a high Himalayan peak.

Visualize planting a mango tree to reap the fruit. A small mud pit is to be dug, and in the early stages, the plant ling is to be protected from animals and trespassers. As the plant grows, nutrition needs to be provided with ample amounts of water and sunlight. The leaves need to be protected from insects and animals. While going through all of these steps in order to reap the fruit, the mango fruit is still going to take its due time to ripen. The fruit is not going to appear later or before the right time of fruition. The time of fruition is determined by the karmic condition of the mango seed. In the same way, the monk – mind creates the space and mentality to accept one's own karmic conditions with ease, as seen in the mango tree example, one can only create a suitable space for the mango tree to grow, but the time of fruition is independent of the space created. When in the world an arrow is shot or a conversation is made, both cannot be reverted back; similarly, one's own karma can never be reverted, good or bad, but one can be aware and prepare themselves to accept and understand those effects.

To develop the monk-mind, one needs to be free from the conditioned mind, which is well established. What factors constitute the conditioned mind and need to be addressed? The conditioned mind is the mind that is conditioned by one's wants rather than needs. These wants or requisites are the requisites of society, the culture one lives in, and the habit patterns related to self-affirmations. It is the illusion of these conditions where one sees permanency in them by identifying one's existence solely defined by these parameters. The roles one plays in life are meant to be perfectly played for a period of time and then need to be shunned with the passage of time. After the realization of the conditioned mind, the mind naturally attenuates to the basic and pure state of mind of stillness and silence, where the karmic conditions are let to unfold with a sense of non-attachment. If any of the karmic conditions are going to anuhow manifest, then why the Monk – Mind? As seen in the mango tree example, the care and nutrition given to it are vital for its fruition. The monk-mind is the creation of a similar type of mental space to accept one's karmic revelations with ease and stability. The conditioned mind is like noise on the radio. One has to go through the noise to arrive at the desired radio frequency. The desired radio frequency is the Monk-Mind frequency. The noise that one has to endure is the noise of the conditioned mind. Since the conditioned mind is always dwelling on the past and the future, it never accepts one's own present. The real answers to the conundrum of life lie deep inside one's consciousness, where one gets apt intuition when stuck at a crossroads. This is the monk-mind, but to reach this state of consciousness, one has to go through the noise and go above the noise of the conditioned mind. As one maneuvers the radio to the destined channel, one has to learn to sail through the conditioned mind to reach the monk-mind, where the noise of the conditioned mind is totally nullified.

The state of the mind is a natural and basic state of mind. It is as obvious as the sun rising in the east, the rivers meeting the ocean, the fruits falling off a tree, and the four seasons of a year. To reach this state of mind, one needs to slowly and patiently be aware of the factors in the mind. The practices and insights over a period of time slowly yet steadily help to be in tandem with the factors of the monk's mind.

The monk – mind is the natural state, which is to be gradually achieved with simple steps and the right intention. Slowly, one becomes aware of the factors of the monk – mind through practice, insight, and the factors of the monk's lifestyle as not to overcome, not to defeat, not to win. Just getting simpler and simpler, quiet and quiet, and becoming one with the bliss of silence.

In the next section, the factors of the monk – mind will be discussed. The factors that bring out the mental space of the silence and tranquility present in cave monasteries and Himalayan Mountain peaks that the monk has access to. These factors are essentially the virtues that lie deep in the realm of human existence. The flowering of virtues in the habit patterns and understanding of the human mentality make the individual simple, naturally calm, and silent. One is able to observe the unfoldment of one's karmic conditions with ease without the presence of the conditioned mind.

Factors of the Monk - Mind

1. Courage

2. Patience

3. Equanimity

4. Non – attachment

5. Love

6. Humility

7. Responsibility

Courage

Courage in the context of the monk-mind mental space isn't meant by the courage a soldier displays in the battle. That chivalric courage is an external quality that is displayed and can differ from person to person according to one's karmic conditions. Courage is seen here as an intrinsic quality that everyone has at their disposal but is unaware of or conscious of due to the hindrance of the conditioned mind. Courage is the bedrock of the monk - mind where it acts as a foundation for the development of all the other factors of the monk - mind. Courage in the context of the monk - mind is the quality by which one can observe and be conscious of the impermanence of one's own self-affirmations. Impermanence is the true nature of the self-affirmations, but due to the constant identification and union of one's existence with the self-affirmations, it causes a manifestation of the illusion of permanence. In the law that rules the world, the reality of impermanence always prevails over the temporary self-affirmed existence; when this happens, it often leads to delusion, pain, and sorrow. The root cause of this neurosis is the absence of the well-developed virtue of courage, which makes one aware of the impermanence of nature in self-affirmations. Courage helps one to be aware of the attachment created by the mind to the self—affirmations.

Self-affirmations are nothing but the flow of one's karmic conditions with respect to time and space, but the attachment to the affirmations makes one think that the totality of one's existence is defined by these affirmations. Courage is the main factor in breaking the mental attachment to these karmic conditions and seeing them as a continuous flow of the effects of past and present actions. In a river flowing, the water at a point in time and place can be said "it is a river" but after a certain change of time and place, the earlier portion of the river cannot be defined in its entirety. So, at no given time and space do the self-affirmations of one entirely describe the existence of oneself. But the illusion caused by the attachment makes one think so. Similarly, like the river, one should be aware of one's different karmic conditions at different points in time and space during one's period of existence. Courage helps one to be aware of the attachment the mind creates to the karmic unfoldment, thus assisting one to glide freely over the karmic conditions that have resulted in different self-affirmations in a natural way without any effort and be free from defilements of anger, sorrow, hatred, and illusion. Courage is the main factor that helps to accept the culmination and origin of different karmic unfoldments. Sometimes there is a gap or pause between two events of karmic conditioning. Courage helps in keeping one at peace and not becoming anxious during that gap period. When there is a gap in the unfoldment of karma, there is an unsettling emotion, which is anxiety. The emotion of anxiety is present due to the ever-present existence of death in life. Death cannot be justified; why does one die? What happens after death? These questions do not have answers that satisfy the human intellect. There are, of course, theories and narratives about what happens after death in religious texts and in the sermons of spiritual teachers, yet they do not completely dispel the darkness surrounding the mystery of death. They do, of course, shed some light. Because the real knowledge of death can only be gained by experiencing it. And the nature of existence is such that no one can experience death totally and come back and relate the experience to society and to oneself. So, the speculation of what happens after death always remains, as does the emotion of anxiety. But with courage, one can recognize death as the true reality of life and accept it in its entirety. The emotion of anxiety gradually subsides, and one is ready and immune enough for the karmic conditions that arise in due time. This anxiety is an emotion that does not have a mental object; it is the root cause of all other defilements, mainly fear. When there is an event of culmination or commencement of the karmic conditions, then the emotion of anxiety has an object; the emotion of anxiety with an mental or physical object is called fear. Courage helps one mitigate the intrinsic emotions of fear and anxiety. Deep inside the mind, the emotion of anxiety exists in each and every person. The quality of courage within oneself helps one adapt to this anxiety. As anxiety does not have a mental object, it can't be explained easily in layman's terms. With the existence of anxiety and an overpowered, conditioned mind, one is always in search of an object for the mind to pacify the emotion of anxiety. This search for an object never ends, as it is done with the conditioned mind. This eventually leads one to be caught up in fear. The development of courage makes the mind free from fear and manages the emotion of anxiety.

With the clash of the monk and the conditioned mind, one is habituated to heed the conditioned mind. The habit patterns make it easy to follow the advice of the conditioned mind. Courage helps one see through the workings of the conditioned mind, overcome the emotions of anxiety and fear, and follow the true calling of the monk - mind. It takes courage to be simple, basic, free, and natural. For example, when an army commander with a large number of troops is serving, all the soldiers and the military hierarchy function according to his orders. People in society too have respect for the army commander, which is a representation of the stars and the badges the commander puts up on his shoulders and chest. This is the self-affirmation of the commander while in service. Yet after the culmination of the service, he is a typical citizen of a country. The expectation of the commander of others to obey his orders and still respect his rank, as in the army days, is due to the illusion of permanence of the self-affirmation, which causes a neurotic effect and leads the commander to be angry and sorrowful. However, if the commander has developed a sense of the intrinsic courage that is being discussed, the commander would observe the culmination of the karmic condition as an army commander and adjust the mental conditions in such a way that being a commander of the army would not describe the person's existence in totality. It is just one part of existence, not the totality of it. And since the time of being a commander has ended, i.e., the karmic conditions of the army have ended, it is time to move on, and with the intrinsic quality of courage, it is easy to wait with courage until the next karmic conditions arise and accept those conditions. This way with a developed sense of courage one can see the impermanence of self-affirmations and develop a sense of immunity to the ever-changing flow of life.

In day-to-day life, it is comfortable to confirm and live up to the parameters set by society. The parameters are about wealth, power, influence, and success. It is also important to understand that the society and culture that dictate them also set the parameters of a spiritual and holistic life. The parameters of external behavioral patterns of spirituality have no relation to true mental development. Thus, by conforming to those parameters, one largely loses focus on the mental states one needs to achieve and again falls into a trap. To avoid this trap, one has to set clear intentions to be simple, free, and natural, i.e., the monk-mind. To avoid this trap while living in the independent cultural spaces of society, the development of the quality of courage makes it possible to set the intention of developing the monk-mind. When true intentions and the parameters of society collide, it inhibits the journey one takes to become simple and natural. For one to be true to the emotions arising from the unfoldment of the karmic conditionings and the situations one experiences, the individual needs courage. For with courage, there is true acknowledgment of the emotions that arise. That is why courage acts as the immunity strength that prevents the conditioned mind and the outside world from getting in the way of the journey one has endured upon achieving the monk-mind. Courage acts as a protection wall from the conditioned mind and the outside world from deterrence for someone on the path of self-transformation. Courage is the main factor where one can be naturally simple, kind, empathetic, and giving to oneself and the habitat surrounding one, as these are the true basic qualities of human nature. The qualities of simplicity, kindness, and empathy are true qualities that lie deep inside the human mental and physical space. When, with courage, one dissects the veil of the conditioned mind, these qualities of humanness arise. These qualities are not to be practiced or shown in an outward fashion, portraying someone's morality, but these are natural and basic qualities that make someone human. To wither away from these qualities is to deviate from humanness, and to understand and cognize one's own behavioral pattern, courage plays a major role. To be kind, empathetic, and giving is not to do a favor for, but it should come naturally, as it is the most basic and intrinsic nature of human existence.

For commonplace interactions and relationships, courage helps one to be understanding and stoic. For example, the development of the monk-mind can be tested in day-to-day interactions and relationships. When there is an interaction between two people, it is actually the confluence of two different karmic conditions trying to find a common ground to ease each other's existence. When a common ground is found, there is harmony, but when a common ground is not in place, it makes way for misunderstandings and misconceptions. And with courage, one is aware of one's own karmic conditions and also cognizant of the fact that the other person is also dealing with their own karmic conditionings. Even if the other person is unaware of their karmic conditionings, one with the intrinsic quality of courage develops an understanding for the other, the understanding being the virtue of patience, which will be pondered in one of the next chapters. When in these dual interactions, events of misunderstandings or confusion spring up, one with courage can understand the difference of vistas between the two, which is the main reason for the miscommunication. There is difference of a reference point from where a situation and experience two people share relate to, even while the intention may be common. In this process of miscommunication, many times the self-affirmations of the people involved get attacked, thus causing anger, frustration, grief, and hatred. But one with a developed mind is aware of the impermanence of one's self-affirmations and is not hurt by the attack on the personal self-affirmation. Courage makes one aware that the karmic conditions of others are not in one's control and no one in this world would be able to change others' karmic conditions, so it would be rather appropriate to position oneself in a manner where the response to the attack to one's self—affirmations by others—can be well handled. The response of the developed monk-mind person is not from the attack on self-affirmation but on the basis of understanding the difference in perception of the situation and the emotion that has arisen from the situation.

With courage as the basis, one because of the monk-mind nature is kind, empathetic, giving, blissful, and simple, not because it is good to be a person with such qualities, but because these are the basic and natural qualities that a human possesses deep down in one's own existence, and the monk-mind excavates them. Courage then reproduces other factors which are discussed ahead which contribute to the development of the monk – mind.

Patience

The happenings in the world, be they physical or mental, all take place within the boundaries of space and time. These are the basic factors that govern the movement of life. The understanding of the time aspect leads to the development of the quality of patience in one. With the basis of courage established, the monk – mind develops the quality of patience.

The unfoldment of the karmic conditions only takes place at the appropriate time and space. The time at which the karmic unfoldment takes place is the present. The virtue of patience develops in one as a quality of living in the present. The conditioned mind has the habit of wavering in the past and the future, but with the development of patience, one is calm and still able to observe one's own karmic conditionings in the present. The effect of the karmic conditions on the mind arises from emotions of happiness, sorrow, and equanimity. But with the development of patience and the understanding of the flow of time, one is able to condition themselves for the change, as the effect of karmic conditions is variable with the time flow, which leads to variability in the emotion related to the mental object of the karmic conditions. If there is an emotion of happiness connected to the karmic conditions, one is able to conceive that state in the present and also be aware of the ever-changing nature of emotions related to it, meaning the object of the karmic conditions that result in happiness also has the potential to arise an emotion of sorrow with respect to the flow of time. Similarly, the emotion related to a karmic condition in the present may arise as an emotion of sorrow, which one is able to conceive in the present state. Patience makes one aware of the potency that the mental object has to bring up an emotion of happiness with respect to the flow of time.

With the conditioned mind, there arises an emotion of expectation, and when expectations are not met, it leads to restlessness, thus creating delusion, sorrow, anger and grief. The understanding of time developed, results in the virtue of patience. The monk-mind understands the play of the conditioned mind, which in turn leads to the development of the wisdom of patience. As patience is developed, one becomes aware that time is the main factor in the karmic unfoldment. Karmic unfoldment rides on the two wheels of time and space. Then one is aware that effort in itself is not sufficient to experience karmic unfoldment. One thing to be aware of is that not all factors are in the hands of the individual. The flow of time cannot be controlled but understood, and it can always be remembered. This awareness and remembrance that time is a main factor in karmic unfoldment and that time is not in individual control is called patience. In the earlier chapter on the mango tree example, it is with individual effort that the sapling is protected and given nutrition, while the tree can bear fruit only at the appropriate time. Protection and nutrition can be seen as individual efforts, but fruition is independent of individual efforts; it depends upon the quality of the seed or, in the world, the karmic conditions.

Karmic unfoldment always translates with respect to time and space; they act as a stage for the play of karma to play. In a play, every actor has to enter or play out the character at a specific time within the script; otherwise, the play loses its flow. Similarly, in life, due to karmic conditions, one has to adopt different self-affirmations with respect to the flow of time. The flow of time is a natural process and not in individual control; the virtue of patience understands this natural process and adapts to different situations accordingly. Patience helps one respond to situations rather than reacting to them. Reaction to a situation, be it mental or physical, is when one understands that all the factors regarding that situation are in individual control, while in response, there is a deep understanding that even though self-effort is in individual control, there are factors that can never be controlled by individual effort, and time is only the answer to the anxiety. With the development of the quality of patience, one is in harmony with the flow of time, understanding the true nature of situations. The approach to situations becomes responsive rather than reactive, as with a responsive nature, a clear mental picture arises, which leads to a clarity of mind, which in turn leads to more peaceful and still mental states.

With the rise of mental factors, according to different situations, the emotions that arise are not favorable to the individual, and with the conditioned mind in play, there is always a reaction to these unfavorable emotions. The absence of response to these emotions, which translate into reactions to situations, leads to more delusion, which converts into sorrow, misery, and even hatred. With patience at the base of understanding, one sees the need to respond rather than react to emotions and situations. The conditioned mind, which creates restlessness due to a lack of patience, is overpowered by the monk-mind, which understands that with the flow of time, situations and emotions change and remains calm and still by letting things play out in their own way. But it is important to understand that patience is not meant by lethargy or sloth; patience comes into play only when self-effort has been practiced to its maximum. When self-effort to its maximum is practiced, one comes to understand the power and limitations of individual control, releasing one from the trap of the conditioned mind, which makes one think that every situation and action is in one's control.

While interacting in the world patience plays an important role in maintaining composure and equanimity. Equanimity is the subject matter of the next chapter. With a developed sense of patience, one manifests the quality of equanimity in oneself. It is understood that the present self – affirmation of oneself—is the result of past actions or karmic conditions that take place in synchronization with the flow of time. This is true not only for one individual but for every being. When one's self-affirmation in the present is attacked, it causes pain and grief and leads one to attack the affirmations of the second person in the conversation. This is a reactive response to a situation that further deepens the miscommunication and makes one uncomfortable in a relationship with the other. But with a developed virtue of patience, one is aware that no one can control the karmic unfoldment for oneself or even the second person in the picture. Both the people involved in the interaction are dealing with their own karmic conditions, and it is not in their control to alter the unfoldment. This leads to a responsive set of minds and makes interactions and relationships easier to process and find common ground. The responsive or patient mind is aware that if all the factors of self-effort are met, then time is the only solution to all the restlessness and delusion that is caused by the conditioned mind.

With the intention of cultivating virtues, one embarks on the path of attaining the monk-mind, and results are not easy to come by. As with one's efforts in the physical world, one can see tangible results, but even to experience tangible results, one has to give time for the results to appear in the space that one has created. As one is in the habit of following the patterns of the conditioned mind, sometimes it is very difficult because the habit formed over years overpowers the natural state of mind. Even though the intention is strong, this habit of following the patterns of the conditioned mind does not diminish that easily. This many a times leads to doubt, and this doubt then leads to aversion on this path of self-transformation. But with the development of the virtue of patience, one understands that karmic conditions are an effect of one's own actions, and to be free from the cusp of the conditioned mind, time is only the solution. Even if one has put in a lot of self-effort to be free from the conditioned mind, self-effort individually does not guarantee emancipation from the workings of the conditioned mind. Self-effort also has to be directed in such a way that it helps in developing the virtue of patience, so when one embarks on this journey of developing the monk-mind, one does not set a pre-meditated time frame. One is aware that this process of transforming into the monk-mind can be a lifelong process, and this thought appears when the virtue of patience is purified and perfected.

One embarks on the journey and observes a shift in mentality from the conditioned mind to the monk-mind. To understand this shift with an example, a person with better economic and financial prospects migrates to another country. Even though the perks of economic and financial prospects are present, one also has to endure and acclimate to the culture, temperature, and geography of the region one has migrated to. But one is strong-headed and only focuses on the economic and financial development and does not adjust oneself to the culture, food habits, and climatic conditions of the new region, and one starts to create a mentality of restlessness and uneasiness. This is due to the strong memory and attachment to the culture and habits of the previous cultural and regional space. But a person with the virtue of patience understands that with every new region come new habits and new cultural dispositions. Slowly and steadily, that person adapts to these new factors with one's own pace of understanding. Similarly, when one embarks on the path of purification, i.e., realizing the monk-mind in the beginning, it becomes difficult to adapt to the new set of mental states, be they internal or external, and more than often, it is frightening. This leads many to revert back to the functioning of the conditioned mind. This often leads to a snake-and-ladder type of situation. One climbs up to the state of the monk-mind but again falls back to the conditioned mind. But someone who has perfected the virtues of courage and patience is aware that one is habituated to the workings of the conditioned mind, and this new territory of the natural state of mind is new. And with new territory come new learnings and new experiences, which vary largely from the earlier states of mind, so to adjust to these new experiences and states of mind, one has to give time to adjust to these new experiences and learnings. Giving time for adjustment is the development of patience, which keeps one on track for self-transformation.

Patience gives one the understanding that reaching the state of the monk-mind is a continuous process, so setting a time frame is of no importance. When there is only the certainty of death, one has to remember, and keeping only death as a frame of reference, one keeps on perfecting the virtues. Just as a monk in caves and Himalayan peaks is sitting in deep meditation, there is no set time frame for life; one in the world or in monastic training has to be free of any time frame for this self-transformation, as the only time set is by the karmic conditionings, and that is death. So, patience is the mindset one aspires to develop, where one till the last breath is on the path of developing the monk-mind. With the understanding of patience, one is free of restlessness and embarks peacefully without any hurriedness on the path of transformation.

Equanimity

With the virtues of courage and patience developed, there arises the quality of equanimity. Equanimity is just awareness of situations and the emotions arising from those situations in the mind. With the virtue of equanimity, there is no labeling of objects, situations, and emotions as good or bad, healthy or unhealthy, or right or wrong. It is the ability one develops to observe the happenings in the mind as they are without judgment. When one is able to observe and accept the happenings in the world and in the mind in their totality, one develops the virtue of equanimity.

Equanimity is the important factor that accelerates the development of the monk – mind. With old habit patterns that have emerged from the workings of the conditioned mind, one is habituated to give into judgments and to the happenings that lead to emotions. A judgmental mind is indicative of a weak mind where the virtues of courage, patience, and equanimity haven't yet developed. As discussed in the earlier chapter, patience is the time factor in the flow of karmic unfoldment. Equanimity creates the space where the karmic unfoldment takes place in a wholesome manner. Wholesome manner here is meant by understanding that one accepts one's self-affirmations as a result of one's actions, and with that comes acceptance of the affirmations in their entirety. With this understanding, there is no judgment about the emotions that arise as pre-mediated expectations are removed in totality. The judgmental mind, which is a manifestation of the conditioned mind, is built upon the conditions of good and bad, right and wrong, personal and non-personal, and so on and so forth. The monk's mind, with its developed sense of equanimity, accepts things as they are in their totality. Totality, meaning equanimity, makes one realize that in this world, nothing is perfect; the idea of utopia is a dream and an illusion. If one situation or the emotion related to the situation is suitable for one, then there is also an opposite emotion that is contained in the totality that has not yet risen. Similarly, if a situation is bad or unfavorable for one, then there is also an opposite emotion that is contained in the totality that has not yet risen. For example, if one is eating a famous delicacy, if it is the first-time experience for the consumer, it is a new experience, and there is no comparison, but if the delicacy consumed in the present has already been consumed by the person beforehand, there is always an unintentional comparison that is going to happen. But a person with developed virtues is always aware of the behavior of the conditioned mind, that is, to compare. But a developed monk-mind treats the two incidents independently and refrains from the comparison. The monk-mind understands the dual nature of existence and refrains from this comparison. This refraining from comparison is developed by the virtue of equanimity. The conditioned mind only focuses on one aspect of the emotion that is tangible to the individual, thus leading one to be afflicted by only one aspect of the situation and the emotion related to it, while the monk-mind helps one with the development of equanimity to be immune to all emotions that have arisen from situations, be they mental or physical. The reason for this mental immunity is the capability of the monk's mind to accept reality in its totality. With equanimity, one develops the capability to accept the dual nature of existence, which is reality and not an illusion.

The conditioned mind has the habit of wandering in the past and future, but with the awareness of reality gained through the virtue of equanimity, it creates the ability for one to focus on the happenings of the present. With the knowledge of reality, one develops a mentality of observing the happenings from a distance without engaging expectations of one to come in between the situations and the emotions that have arisen from them. This non-engagement mentality with respect to expectations is the result of the virtue of equanimity. This mentality then reduces pain, fear, sorrow, and grief caused by the association of one's expectations with the happenings of reality.

With the acceptance of reality, one is less engaged in reversing it with the virtue of equanimity. When one develops the virtue of equanimity, one guides one's energies into adapting to different emotions and situations rather than trying to change the object or situation that has risen. This adaptive mentality is the answer to one's difficulties. The absence of judgment facilitates one not to associate with the emotions arising from situations and objects in the mental space.

The awareness that the flow of karmic conditions with time results in different situations and mental spaces, and the awareness that the flow of karma and its effects are not in one's control, enhances the development of the virtue of equanimity. This gives rise to a wholesome state of mind, and this wholesome state of mind gives rise to a sense of freedom. This internal sense of freedom makes one believe and grow in faith on the path of the development of the monk – mind. With the development of equanimity, it helps one to attract a positive state of mind. This positive state of mind helps one concrete oneself on this path. This rising above the duality of existence makes one move onto developed states of mind where there is perennial peace and stability. Rising above situations and emotions only happens when there is knowledge of the existence of duality, and equanimity as a virtue provides the right space for freedom from attachment to the emotions and objects of existence. This rising above mentality from the emotions makes one understand the emotions of anxiety and fear. As anxiety is consistent with one's existence, the freedom manifested by the virtue of equanimity makes one mitigate all fears and anxieties. This happens because equanimity prevents one from being associated with all types of emotions and conditions. This is the true nature of freedom and a wholesome state of mind.

In common-world interactions Equanimity plays an essential role in creating a wholesome space where individuals can co-exist in an understanding manner. The role of expectations has ceased, which had been created by the conditioned mind. Expectations not only from the self—existing karmic conditions—but also from another individual are a major cause of sorrow, grief, and miscommunication. Equanimity creates awareness of the duality present in the existence of reality. When an emotion or experience based on the behavior of a person arises, one is aware that the present emotion is not the entirety of the emotion based upon that interaction or experience. There is also a divergent experience that has not come into play but has the potential to rise up with the course of time; this awareness makes one adjust to reality. As discussed in the earlier chapter, it makes one not react but adjust accordingly to the reality of life. This virtue of equanimity, when well-developed, creates a mental and physical space of silence. Thus, equanimity is the root virtue of developing silence. Forced silence without awareness of the nature of reality does not last long, but for a developed mental state, silence becomes the true nature of existence. Silence creates space for one's karmic conditions to play out smoothly, in the sense that there is no addiction or aversion to the karmic unfoldment. It becomes a natural phenomenon just as the sun rises every morning, water flows down a mountain, and fire rises up into the sky. With silence based on the virtue of equanimity, one only has to experience the karmic unfoldment based on past actions. But with the presence of silence based on equanimity, one does not create a new balance of karmic conditions. As one ceases creating new karmic conditions, one is truly emancipated, i.e., the monk-mind has totally developed in one. But it is important to understand that even though a new karmic balance is not created, one is only totally free after total exhaustion of the past karmic conditions. With this silence, it is not meant that one does not engage in conversation and stops contemplating or thinking. Silence is the cessation of the emotion or habit of expectation. When the blanket of expectation covering the true nature of equanimity is extracted, then the beauty of silence is experienced. This is the true meaning of silence; silence or equanimity is not confirmed by inaction or emotionlessness. Actions or emotions expressed with a true understanding and awareness of the nature of existence are the silence of equanimity.

Two individuals are friends, and this friendship has been lasting for a long time. The emotions that arise from a friendship relationship are understanding, care, affection, and empathy. The root cause of the friendship that has resulted in the rise of these emotions is a subtle synchronization of each other's karmic conditions. And with the passage of time, the bond of friendship grows stronger. As time passes, there is also a possibility that the synchronization of each other's karmic conditions ceases to exist, and there arise emotions exactly opposite to those that were built on the basis of friendship. Similarly, when there is enmity between two individuals, the enmity gives rise to emotions of hatred, anger, and jealousy. This is due to the fact that the karmic conditions of the two individuals are not in synchronization. But with the flow of time, there is definitely a change in the karmic conditions of the two, and the new conditions have the potency to convert enmity into friendship. This, with an example, was meant by the dual nature of the existence of the world. An individual with a developed monk-mind is aware of the duality of the nature of existence. With the presence of the conditioned mind, one is not aware of the dual nature of existence due to the nature of expectations. With the developed virtue of equanimity, one is aware of this dual nature. This awareness makes one adjust, rise above the emotions that have risen, and observe their working independently rather than getting worked by the emotions. This virtuous mind does not get worked up by emotions that arise but observes their working independently; this is the essence of equanimity. It helps one to choose emotions according to their will to move on the path of the monk-mind rather than getting worked on by emotions that arise with time. Does this mean that, with the dual nature of existence, we treat a friend as an enemy and an enemy as a friend? That would be a fallacy. But it surely points out, in the direction where one is aware of this dual nature, that in friendship lies a dormant existence of enmity, and in enmity lies a dormant existence of friendship based on the synchronization of karmic conditions. When the roles get reversed with the flow of time, one does not get afflicted with the reverted emotions that have risen. One is also aware that all the emotions that have risen are impermanent and purely depend upon the karmic unfoldment. This natural state of mind, with this awareness, is the basis for creating a healthy and wholesome mental space. This mental space leads to silence and true positivity. This silence leads to stability and manifestation of higher mental states and furthers one's faith in the path of the monk-mind. With equanimity as the basis, one develops the quality of non-attachment, the virtue that defines the monk-mind.

Non – Attachment

The general notion of non-attachment is visualized as a skinny monk with ragged clothes with no interest in living. But the monk-mind is a developed state of wholesome mental and physical states. Monk-mind can be visualized as a recreation of the healthy mental states of monks living in developed states of existence. These are true monks who have understood the essence and truth of living. There is no running away, as fear and anxiety have been conquered by understanding their true existence. Monkhood and monk-mind are truly different aspects. Monkhood is usually just the outward portrayal of being a monk, while a true monk's mind is the real, developed mind based on virtues. Monkhood is only true when it is the true representation of a developed monk-mind. Without developed virtues in the mind, monk hood also becomes an illusion, as the self-affirmation of being a monk is not based on the reality of existence; it is just another affirmation one confirms to be permanent, as in the physical material world. This gives a contradictory understanding of non-attachment, as non-attachment is the virtue on which the workings of the monk-mind thrive. Non-attachment is often confused with non-caring, selfishness, and contempt for existence. These behaviors and emotions are a product of anxiety, fear, and illusion. Anxiety, fear, and illusion can never be the basis of the monk-mind but form a mentality polar opposite to it. And with this, non-attachment can only be flaunted superficially rather than becoming a natural state of being. With the developed virtues of courage, patience, and equanimity comes the virtue of non-attachment. Non-attachment is the virtue that differentiates a truly developed mind from a conditioned mind. With the wholesome mental space created by the virtue of equanimity and with the development of non-attachment, one ceases to associate oneself in entirity with the karmic conditions. The association of oneself is the association of the conditioned mind with the situations and emotions that have arisen from karmic conditions. Attachment is the attachment of habit patterns, expectations, and resolutions of the past and future to present situations and emotions. To observe the happenings of the past, present, and future independently and cease the overlapping of the conditioned mind over these happenings is the development of the virtue of non-attachment. With the developed virtue of non-attachment, one focuses one's energies on the happenings of the present without the conditionings of past happenings and also without the expectations of future happenings. This is because the self-affirmations are a result of the karmic conditions and do not need to overlap with the present happenings. A true monk-mind with a developed mental state is full of zest and energy for the happenings in the present. With the absence of past volitions and future expectations, there arises an emotion of bliss to enjoy the present.

To be free from the expectation of a particular result from situations and emotions is to remove attachment. One has fixations on the behavior and workings of situations. These fixations are caused by habit patterns arising from past experiences and memories. Self-affirmations are thought to be permanent with these fixations. Thus, the illusion caused by these fixations heaps expectations on behavior and the consequences of emotions and events. These fixations make one stuck in the flow of time and karmic unfoldment. This virtue of non-attachment is to be free from the fixation of the permanency of self-affirmations. The ability to let go of desired emotions, events, and consequences is non-attachment. When one thinks that the present self-affirmation is the entirety of one's existence, it brings in these expectations of behavioral patterns. A reputed doctor in a famous hospital is habituated to a certain behavioral pattern in the hospital that is one of respect and adulation, but this respect and adulation necessarily does not translate into another space, for example, at home or at the supermarket. At home, the doctor's self-affirmations are of being a son, a father, or a husband. Similarly, in the supermarket, the doctor is just another customer for a vendor. The affirmation of the doctor that only revolves around being a doctor in the entirety of existence is the fixation of the self, which causes delusion, anger, and sorrow. The fixation may also translate to one's spiritual practices, faith, culture and religion. This fixation does not let the individual flow with the different self-affirmations with the flow of time. The expectation that all the spheres of existence should treat the person as a doctor is the cause of defilements. But with the virtue of non-attachment, the person is not fixated on just one role but glides through different roles and, with awareness, is able to see the impermanence. Just as a person changes clothes every day for sanity and hygiene purposes, non - attachment as a virtue allows an individual to glide through one's affirmations with ease for the sanity and hygiene of the mental space. With the developed virtue of non-attachment, one is free from the fixations of the past and the future. It is a feeling of freedom when a heavy boulder is removed from one's shoulders. With this lightness of mind, one is then able to live in the present.

With awareness of the certain possibility of death, one is able to practice non-attachment with more ease. As the past habits of the conditioned mind always create a block in the free flow of life, contemplation on death always acts as a true reminder of the impermanence of the self—affirmations, thus helping one to give in to the flow of life.

Thus, non-attachment gives rise to a mentality of renunciation. Renouncing not the world, family, responsibilities, or karmic conditions but the subtle renouncing of the mentality of fixation of one's self—affirmations. This renunciation of the fixation of the mind is true renunciation, and according to one's own karmic conditions, one can either practice it while living in the world or as a monk practicing deep in the forest. But the important factor is to develop renunciation on the basis of non-attachment. This renunciation is the cause of bliss and the ability to live life more naturally and in a simplistic manner.

In worldly interactions and relationships, non-attachment creates a clear space for identification of one's influence on the other. This understanding of influence helps one to be free of expectations set for the other person. Getting rid of expectations makes relationships last longer. On the basis of the virtue of non-attachment, the nature of relationships transcends from a transactive nature to an accommodative nature. This accommodative or supportive nature of relationships leads to faith and the development of the emotion of love between the corresponding individuals. With faith and love established between individuals as the true nature of existence, life becomes easy to live, and there is a subtle joy in living in the world. No one can deny the fact that humans are social beings. And living happily in society on the basis of love and faith for every individual is a skill. This skill is mastered through the development of the virtue of non-attachment. In situations, non-attachment converts into the philosophy of living and letting live. Living means that one is totally aware of the present without being attached to the conditions of the past and the future. Letting live means that one does not superimpose their own karmic conditions or expectations on the other. Why should the other person carry another individual's karmic conditions? That is not the duty, as it overburdens the second person. This overburdening becomes the root cause of tensions in relationships. If a person is helping another individual based on love and empathy, it is justified, but the second person who is being helped should not take the help for granted, as the conditioned mind makes one think and take the help for granted. This makes living and maintaining healthy relationships difficult. The awareness that everyone is adapting to their own karmic conditionings and needs to be supported or helped rather than getting help from others slowly cultivates in the individual with the development of this virtue. One accepts the help and understanding received from others as a gift based on gratitude rather than presuming help and understanding from others as a birthright. This leads to an accommodative nature of mind, where everyone, whether they understand or behave in a suitable manner or not, is not of major consequence. But the significance lies in the understanding that, with the unfoldment of karmic conditions, a series of self-affirmations arise. The self-affirmations come with a set of duties and actions. With the understanding of non-attachment, one performs duties and actions independent of the conditioned mind. That is, one performs all the actions with total awareness of the present. There is also an understanding that these actions are being taken for the culmination of the karmic conditions, and the second person has no role in them. If the role is favorable, it is a gift from past and present actions, and if the role is not favorable, it is also a situation arising from past and present actions. This virtue of non-attachment gives rise to being grateful for the favorable interactions and a sense of equanimity for the not-so-favorable ones. This is because of the awareness that one only reaps the reward of the seeds one sows. A person playing the role of a father brings up his child. He educates, gives the child love and care, teaches about the workings of society, and acts as a strong support system. Similarly, the child looks up to the father for advice, support, and love. With the virtue of non-attachment, the father makes the child an independent adult with good values and a better citizen of the world. He helps his child to be the best version of itself; the child is also naturally grateful for the father's care, love, and affection. This affection is shown by being there for the father during his old age, spending quality time with the parent, and making sure that the father leads a comfortable life. But if the quality of non-attachment is not developed, the father envisions the child as an investment for the future. When the child becomes independent, it may be another source of income; if the child becomes successful, as a parent, it is a big benefit for the social status; so on and so forth. Also, the child sees the parent as a liability and discards his existence. The nature of the relationship also becomes transactional, where the child has an eye on the property or wealth of the parent. This virtueless living is a major cause of delusion, sorrow, and hatred, even in relationships with close ones. But the nature of the monk's mind is to be as simple as possible. The monk-mind helps one understand that to be simple and natural is to develop the virtue of non-attachment, where one does duties and performs actions without any expectation from the second person. One performs duties because it is the most humane thing to do, and to perform actions and duties with the developed virtue of non-attachment is to be free from these duties. No one is doing favors for anybody for performing their actions and duties with diligence; it is one's prerogative to do so even if the other person involved is supportive or not. With this virtue developed, even while living in the world, one can manifest higher and more peaceful states of mind. These virtues of courage, patience, equanimity, and non-attachment, when manifested to their highest potentials, help in harvesting even higher characteristics like renunciation, love, gratitude, and humility.

Love

The practice and development of non-violence in daily life is love. Non-violence means non-harming with actions, speech, and mental factors. The virtue of love for the monk-mind is primarily to love oneself first. To love oneself is to understand the practice of non-violence in action, speech, and mind. The root of all actions and speech are mental factors. The synchronization of the mind, action, and speech is true love for oneself. When one distances oneself by disowning one's own karmic conditions, one starts violating one's own existence. This non-acceptance of all the mental factors due to one's own conditioned mind leads to a disruption in the synchronization of the mind, action, and speech. This is meant by self-love, i.e., accepting one's own existence in its entirety.

A gap is created in the rejection of the karmic conditions or the present state of existence. This gap, or void, is filled by the conditioned mind. When the conditioned mind takes over the natural state of mind, one starts violating the beauty of self-existence. This is the nature of self-hatred. One has to be aware that one's existence in the world has some purpose attached to it. The conditioned mind engulfs the true purpose of life, which has been premediated by the existence of karmic conditions. This engulfing is done with past volitions and habit patterns. This unawareness of one's true purpose in life or the reason for existence is a violation of individual existence. This is the main concern for the absence of self-love. With the acceptance of oneself in its entirety, that is, acceptance of all the karmic conditions, one becomes aware of the true purpose of life. Understanding the true purpose of life is an easy task, but the habit patterns of the conditioned mind come in between and make the task difficult. To understand and be aware of the real purpose of life is to be in love with oneself. This acceptance of the entirety of karmic conditions and then the awareness of the real purpose of one's own existence leads to synchronization of one's thoughts, actions, and speech. When this trinity becomes synchronized, the purpose of life gets clearer, just as the sun gets brighter as the clouds move away. This synchronized trinity is the effect of the monk – mind. The synchronization of mind, speech, and actions is the true nature, or the basic nature, of the mind. When this synchronization manifests, it is concluded that one has developed the simple and natural state of mind, or the monk-mind. This simple and natural state of mind is perfectly able to reflect on the true purpose of life, as intended by existence. When this true reflection of the intention of one's existence takes place in the mental space, one embarks on the journey of loving oneself in a true manner. With this reflection of intention in one, there is an immense flow of energy to live life to the fullest.

What is the true purpose for one as intended by existence? The purpose of existence could be understood with an example. A banyan tree seed germinates into a sapling; from a sapling, it grows into a small tree, and with due course of time, it grows into a large tree with many branches and a strong girth, and the tree bears fruits. The purpose of the seed was that it needed to be transformed into a fruit-bearing tree. The process of self-transformation has been completed after fruition. But the transformation in itself was to provide for the world or existence. The fruition of the tree eventually has to do with facilitating life forms in existence. The tree acts as a support system for birds to build nests, and the leaves are food for many insects and ants. The soil under the tree becomes nutritional, and many animals and even humans take shelter under the tree. The fruits of the tree can be used as medicine and for nutrition. An ecosystem of living beings starts to develop and depend on and around the tree. This is the natural purpose of the tree. This is the real intention of nature for the tree that has been accomplished by the seed. The seed has the true knowledge of intention imbibed by its existence. There are no conditions that hinder the natural growth that exists inside the seed. With due course of time, the true intention is accomplished when a wholesome space is created for the seed. Only with its simple existence has the tree been giving back to nature, and even while doing that, there is no expectation of any return. There is no notification of the services provided by the tree. This is the true nature of love. There is only giving back to existence without any expectation of a receipt.

It is because of the natural flow of energy in the tree that an ecosystem of living beings lives rent-free and benefits from the existence of the tree. Similarly, like the tree, human existence also has an intention naturally set by its existence. The conditioned mind comes in the way of that awareness, and human existence spirals into a downfall with lower states of mentality. But with awareness of the intention set by existence, there arises a need to act on this true intention; this act becomes the duty set by nature for this lifetime. The intention is to develop wholesome and higher mental states, and with the development of these higher and wholesome mental states, one becomes aware of the true intentions set by existence. The duty set with these intentions is to facilitate life not only for one's own self but for existence as a whole. As the tree facilitates an ecosystem of life surrounding itself, similarly, the fruition of human mental space is to spread the seeds of wisdom in society or existence in a natural way. The natural way is the way of the monk-mind, where following and practicing the virtues becomes a way of life rather than a superficial imposition. With this natural mental space, one becomes a divine instrument for the natural energies to flow. And with the flowing of these evergreen energies, there will be transformation of the self, the people surrounding the transformed self, the nation of the transformed self, and the universe as a whole. This is the true nature of human existence and the purpose intended for it. With this flow of natural energies, there is only the act of giving left in one. This giving is without any expectations, and giving on the basis of non-attachment to any expectations is the true basis of love. This is the highest form of love. When one only starts giving to and for existence, it starts providing the individual with energy and deeper knowledge. These knowledge and energies help one attain higher states of existence. When one is aware of the true intention set by existence and acts on the intention with the mind, it manifests into synchronization of mind, speech, and action. This synchronization is the essence of love, which is actually a giving attitude. When the trinity acts, its synchronization leads to the act of giving selflessly. This is the fruition of love in the self.

The fruition of the virtue of love translates into action and behavioral patterns. The actions and behavioral patterns then convert themselves into stronger and deeper relationships. The emotion of love in the world is usually seen as a depiction of superficial intimacy based on mere physical and material arrangements. This is an attraction. Attraction and love should not be misunderstood as one. Attraction is the virtue one develops as a result of the workings of the conditioned mind. Attraction is a temporary understanding of another's existence. It never lasts long. The quality of attraction decreases as the newness of the relationship decreases with time. With the decrease in newness comes boredom. Boredom creates lethargy and carelessness. Lethargy and carelessness are qualities of an underdeveloped mind. Attraction has no relationship with the intention of awareness. Attraction only rises when the virtue of awareness is not perfected. With a lack of awareness, the individual gives in to the habit patterns of the conditioned mind. It labels objects and situations and relates them to the happenings of self-existence. This arrangement is the work of the conditioned mind, where there is a strong attachment to expectations. There is always a foundation of wants and needs for a relationship; this is the foundation of the conditioned mind. One expects the other person in a relationship to behave in a particular way that is suitable for satisfying the needs of the other person in the relationship. There is a dearth of selflessness in the relationship. This aloofness created by a lack of selflessness is the root cause of misunderstanding and dishonesty. When two individuals are in love, they actually create a physical and mental space where each one can grow in understanding, simplicity, and selflessness. The true joy is in making each other's lives simple and easy rather than expecting the other to do it for the other person. The mere existence of one for the other is ample for one to be happy and content. When mere presence without any conditions is enough for each other to feel safe and cared for, that is true love in a practical sense. This only happens when individuals create a wholesome mental and physical space where they can deal with their own karmic unfoldment without any judgment. There is a deep understanding of each other's mental and physical requirements so that the ability to face the karmic conditionings can be developed. As immunity to karmic conditions develops, the bond between the individuals becomes subtler. It penetrates from the more physical realms to the mental realms. There happens a beautiful surrendering to each other's existence where all the questions die down and the mere beauty of the silence of being in each other's existence arises.

The qualities with which love prospers are surrender and selflessness. These qualities need to be purified or perfected to understand the deeper aspects of love in existence. The quality of selflessness needs to be purified in such a way that one observes a reflection of oneself in the totality of existence. There are no two individuals in the equation. When one sees only one self in the totality of existence, how can there be any place for any violence? How can one be violent toward oneself? There is an experience of oneness everywhere. This experience of oneness only happens when one is aware, as one is trying to adjust to one's own karmic conditions and so are the other individuals in existence. This awareness brings an understanding of the oneness of existence. Surrender is the quality of dissolving one's own conditioned mind. As a pinch of salt totally dissolves in a glass of water and one cannot differentiate water from salt, when one dissolves the conditioned mind in totality and only the natural or monk-mind remains, the quality of surrender is perfected. The surrender happens when one develops the understanding that the karmic conditions are not in individual control, so one lets go of the controlling mindset of the conditioned mind. With the dissolution of the conditioned mind, only the intentions and actions expected by its existence take place, just as a free-flowing river meets the sea. It is as natural as the virtue of non-violence becomes so natural that violence seems like a far-fetched thought. Nobody would be able to force one to practice or undertake violent actions. Not only one with a developed virtue of love can bear the pain of sorrow and despair of close and loved ones, but also for the existence of the whole.

One gives a hand of support and help to all as one's true nature, rather than a superficial show of these qualities. This is the true nature of human existence, which separates human mentality from lower mental states of existence. Love is the bond that unifies all of existence, and with the real human mentality, one knows nothing more than that but to practice it.

Humility

Humility is the virtue by which one walks the path of the monk-mind. With humility as a defense mechanism, the conditioned mind rarely attacks. Humility always makes one aware of the conditioned mind. Individuals striving for better and higher mental states generally end up being arrogant. Arrogance is usually the main reason for the downfall. The downfall here is the conditioned mind taking over the workings of the mind. Arrogance rises when one starts seeing the development of the mind. Yet one is not aware of the monkey-like nature of the mind. It does not take a lot of time to fall into the lesser mental states. Overcoming the actions and the workings of the conditioned mind through understanding is a time-consuming and rigorous process. It takes a lot of energy for a rocket to escape the gravitational pull to reach space, but no extra energy is required for the rocket to fall back to the ground. Reaching the monk-mind state is a rigorous process, while falling back to the workings of the conditioned mind is effortless. One assumes that once a higher mental state is reached, it is forever, but it is not so. The mind is very clever at making one think so. The development of the mind is a never-ending process. The only full stop one can relate to is death. Even though death is just a comma, one can rest and not think at the time of the event. The assumption that the higher mental or monk-mind states are permanent has emerged from the workings of arrogance.

Arrogance usually leads to wants and needs. The desire for respect and the desire for power and influence are what arrogance leads to. There is a lack of understanding between the existence of the self and the existence of the whole because of arrogance. The only remedy that ceases the springing up of arrogance is humility. Humility acts as a constant reminder when defilements like arrogance arise. The reminder is to be aware of these unwholesome workings of the conditioned mind. With this constant reminder of the virtue of humility, one is aware, and with this awareness, one remains focused on the path of the monk – mind. The awareness provided by the virtue of humility acts as a shield for one from the attacks of arrogance. Humbler the individual, longer gets the spell of the monk-mind. Humility puts one in check if the conditioned mind resumes it's working and suggests one keep the head low and let the focus be on the constant awareness of the virtues of the monk – mind.

A plant or a tree laden with fruit is always bent toward the ground, while plants or trees lacking fruits are always seen to be rising toward the sky. The fruits laden on the tree are the virtues of courage, patience, equanimity, non-attachment, and love. An individual who has really cultivated these virtues and has reaped their fruition automatically becomes down to earth with the virtue of humility. On the other side, arrogance is the mentality developed by a person who is empty of such virtues. The inability to develop virtues is the root cause of developing unwholesome states of existence. Thus, one becomes arrogant, loud-mouthed, and even boastful. It is the powerlessness of developing virtues that is being transformed into these lesser mental states. These lesser mental states belong to the conditioned mind. When the virtues of life do not become a natural part of one's existence, one makes an effort to artificially superimpose them. This artificial superimposition is the cause of all the arrogance and self-righteousness. The inability makes one give rise to an inferiority complex. This complex makes one's existence feel null and void. This feeling is the very cause of fear and anxiety. To blanket the feelings or emotions of anxiety and fear, one needs to cling on to the thought of permanency of self-affirmations. These affirmations are then communicated through the acts and emotions of arrogance and self-righteousness. Humility is the true weapon with which one is able to cut through or wade through these vices.

However, humility and arrogance are opposite emotions. Humility can be misunderstood for a lack of self-respect. Humility is actually the highest respect for the existence of an individual. But usually, self-respect is confused with arrogance. It is important to be aware of the fact that both are very different emotions. Self-respect is a wholesome state of mind, while arrogance and stubbornness are vices that emerge from the conditioned mind. The virtue of humility makes one confident in one's existence, as there is nothing to hide from. There is an awareness that there is a certain beauty existing in each and every being in existence. One is able to accept the vices and the positives one is in possession of. There is also beauty in one's existence, irrespective of the mental states one has achieved. But with the development of the virtue of humility, one is able to accept and appreciate this beauty. This acceptance and appreciation of the virtue of humility helps one work on oneself. The misunderstanding that humility as a lack of self-respect can be eliminated by accepting one's own vices and positives, and an understanding that the path of the monk-mind is never-ending and the process of constant self-transformation is never-ending, then there is no effect of higher states of being and lower states of being on one. One has understood it is a continuous journey. The understanding that everyone is on this journey and that at each point of existence there lies a certain beauty of existence emerges as an emotion or quality of regard and respect for the entirety of existence. This respect and regard are built on the foundation of humility.

A true monk is always humble. A true monk is an individual with a developed monk-mind. Humility always guides the way of existence of the monk. In the world, everyone is habituated to look up to someone in the early stages of development. One can either look up to parents, teachers, friends, a guru, and so on and so forth. But certainly, a stage comes in life where, with enough experience, one develops a certain knowledge and wisdom base. This knowledge and wisdom base is, of course, very useful and helpful for individuals trying to work their way up the knowledge path. With the building up of a knowledge and wisdom base, there comes the thought that this knowledge base is sufficient for the remaining part of existence or survival. This makes the knowledge and wisdom from experiences stagnant. This also creates a habit pattern where one thinks that one has the authority to instruct, give orders, openly criticize, or voice opinions. To remove this stagnancy, one has to develop the virtue of humility at all times. In life, it is important that one is looked upon for advice and instructions; it is even more important that one has someone or some qualities and virtues to look up to. This makes one rooted in reality rather than wavering in a dream of respect and adulation. One has to be aware that one is always a student of life. This attitude of a pupil always needs to be developed and cultivated. The quality of inquisitiveness helps one to maintain and develop the virtue of humility for longer and more sustained periods. With this inquisitiveness, knowledge and wisdom have no expiration date. There is always an update to this wisdom and knowledge bank; this only happens when the student-like behavior with inquisitiveness is always maintained. As time and space change, the knowledge and wisdom base require updating; one cannot repeat and bank only on the past knowledge. The basis of wisdom and knowledge always needs to be purified and adjusted to the needs and wants of space and time. Humility, which gives rise to a mentality of inquisitiveness, and student-like behavior create a wholesome mental space for the purification and nurturing of the knowledge base.

What is it that one has to look up to? One could look up to a teacher who has always supported one in understanding life; it could be parents or a guru who has supported one's spiritual journey. If someone confirms a religion, it could be a god or a teacher of that corresponding religion. It does not matter who one looks up to; what matters is the development of humility, which then transcends all of existence. It is the formation of a habit of bowing down in gratitude and thankfulness. Then to whom would a monk meditating in the tall peaks and cave monasteries be humble? The monk in that mental space is humble or looks up to nature or existence. By nature, or existence, it can be understood as the sun, moon, rivers, earth, sky, mountains, and the air one breathes, etcetera. The true monk always takes refuge in the existence as a whole, as the monk is aware that these are the true factors that keep one alive and nurture the awareness even more. Nature, in reality, is the true teacher of life. It only gives to human existence without any expectation of any return; that is what makes nature special. There is always more to learn from nature or existence, as the power of nature supersedes the limited cognitive powers of the human mind. This creates an expansive mental space where one accepts to bow down to the creation and be thankful and grateful for one's own existence. This gratefulness arises from the realization that existence has given one the opportunity to experience one's own karmic conditions, whether good or bad, and at the same time to learn and adapt to be free from their influence. This is the basis of the humility of a truly developed monk – mind. There is no dependence on artificial or mental creations for gratitude. The deep sense of gratitude roots in reality, which is nature or existence. This attitude has to be replicated in the mentality of everyone, be it a monk or a regular office worker.

Humility arises from the learning that one is a sum total of one's own created karmic conditions. There are no real factors outside the realm of one's own karma that determine one's affirmations and way of existence. With this knowledge, one develops a sense of humility for the karmic conditions one has created. This is true humility, as the basis of humility is reality. This prevents one from being arrogant and boastful during the good times and sorrowful and bitter during the not-so-favorable times. These realizations make one follow the path of the monk-mind for a long time while remaining focused on developing virtues.

In front of existence or nature, no one is as powerful. It is in the greater good of the individual to remain humble, as it is a reflection of the individual's humanity. With the awareness that existence and nature are above all else, there is an automatic shift in mentality toward surrendering to existence and nature. This surrender then creates a wholesome mental state of perpetual humility. Humility in practice translates into gratitude for self-existence, the people surrounding the individual, the relationships emerging from the people, and nature as a whole. The emotions arising from relationships with people and with nature in hindsight may be favorable for one or not, but they are not of major concern. The development of humility treats each and every experience and emotion as a way to transcend one's own karmic conditions, and with this awareness, the head bows down in gratitude for the chance provided by existence to navigate through the karmic unfoldment. This leads to true and total emancipation.

Responsibility

A true monk with developed facilities of the mind is aware of self-affirmations. These self-affirmations are a result of the karmic unfoldment. The true monk realizes the importance of the existence of these self-affirmations as well as being aware of their impermanent nature. The predicament that arises in the mind is that if the nature of the self-affirmations is impermanent, then how does one navigate one's existence through them? How does one take on these different roles with the right mindset? With the awareness of the impermanence of these self-affirmations, there is usually a misconception that the roles and duties of these self-affirmations have to be neglected. The neglection of discharging the duties and roles of the self—affirmations—propels many into leaving the world and entering deep into forests and mountain peaks, while at the same time creating a distaste for living a meaningful life. The management of one's mind in a way where there is no thought of neglection and yet there is an awareness of the impermanence of self-affirmation is the true development of the virtue of responsibility in the monk's mind. As the thought of permanence is a product of the conditioned mind, so is the thought or factor of neglection. The main aim of the virtues developed by the monk—mind—is to be free from the conditioned mind. Responsibility as a virtue provides a middle path between the mental conditions of neglect and the view of permanence. If an individual leaves the world and the duties related to living in the world and moves into deep forests or mountain peaks with the misconception of neglecting the duties the self-affirmations have to offer, then this is not becoming a true monk.

The present state of existence of the individual is the result of past actions or karmic conditionings. These karmic conditionings are the result of one's own actions and perceptions from the past. The sown seed of past actions has ripened into the present; there are no external factors that affect the present; however, the karmic conditionings of the past affect the state of one's internal as well as external existence in the present. Internal existence is meant by the mental conditions of one, while external existence is meant by relationships and behavioral patterns. It is important to note that external conditions are a reflection of one's state of internal being. Internal existence is understood by the state of an evolved mind one possesses. This state of the evolved mind is then reflected in its external existence. That is the existence of relationships with health, money, people, situations, etcetera. This realization brings about the true realization of the virtue of responsibility. The awareness that what one does today is due to one's own existence and that tomorrow is going to be the unfolding of the actions of the present. This awareness makes one realize the importance of the virtue of responsibility in the present. Responsibility, then, does not become a burden but becomes a way to be free from conditioning. There is an emotion of love attached to the true meaning of responsibility. The thought of "I should do this" gets converted into "I have to do this." One takes on the responsibilities with gusto to grow in understanding of the present. A total immersion takes place in the duties of self-affirmation, but the immersion is with the awareness that the nature of self-affirmation is not permanent. The immersion of individual existence into the duties of self-affirmation with the awareness of impermanence is the true monk-mind virtue of responsibility.

To be really emancipated from self-affirmations, one has to totally immerse themselves in the duties of self-affirmations. With this immersion, the true knowledge of self-affirmation arises. The totality of the self—affirmation—arises. This knowledge of the totality of self-affirmation is truly responsible for total emancipation from self-affirmation. What if emancipation does not take place? Is it really required to be free from one's own karmic conditioning? The answer lies in the fact that existence has a bigger objective set for the individual, but if the individual is not free from one's own karmic conditionings, how can one be a part of the play of a larger existence? It is important to know that the self-affirmations of the self are a limited set of conditionings that do not fulfill the entire potency of human existence. That is the true aim of existence in the human realm; this aim is to be achieved with the awakening of the monk—mind in one. The true responsibility is fulfilling the aim of the existence set for the human individual by the existence as a whole. This true responsibility cannot be fulfilled until emancipation from the karmic conditions of oneself. To emancipate oneself from one's own karmic conditioning is to immerse oneself in the duties of the self—affirmations. If there is a halfhearted effort into the duties of the self-affirmations, then the conditionings do not completely cease to exist. The remanent part, because of the half-heartedness, makes the individual again fall into experiencing the finite boundaries of one's own conditionings. As it is important to immerse oneself in the duties, it is also important to be aware of the impermanence of the self-affirmations. As with the immersion into the duties of self-affirmation, one gets comfortable living in the self-created realm of existence. But once awareness of impermanence arises, one is able to move on. This helps one to be totally emancipated from all the karmic conditionings.

With the awakening of the true virtue of responsibility, the habit of the conditioned mind to blame external factors for the state of one's existence ceases. The habit of the conditioned mind is to blame others as external factors for the state of one's existence. When the state of one's existence is not favorable, the conditioned mind tends to blame the present state on external factors. And when the state of present existence is favorable, the individual who is governed by the workings of the conditioned mind takes credit for one's own actions. This ironic behavior is the true representation of the conditioned mind. When the circumstances are favorable, it is the individual effort that becomes the major factor, while when the circumstances are unfavorable, external factors are responsible for it. This state of partial acceptance is not what true responsibility means. Responsibility is the acceptance of all the circumstances that arise as a result of one's own actions, be they past or present.

When the circumstances are favorable, one should remember that these favorable conditions are a result of the karmic conditionings of the individual and have no relation to the present state of the individual self. So, when the favorable state of existence appears in the present, one with the true virtue of responsibility is aware that the present state of a favorable state of existence is a gift of past karmic conditionings. This awareness makes one not get too attached to these favorable states. The attachment to favorable states of existence is due to the conditioned mind making one describe one's existence in totality in the present state. The favorable states of existence lead to an intoxicated state of existence; the intoxication is due to the factors that favor one's existence. The favorable factors are those that favor the conditioned mind and are mainly those of comfort of living, good health, social influence, financial power, and so on and so forth. The virtue of responsibility does not negate these factors but makes sure that one has gratitude for these favorable factors, which are a result of one's past actions. There is also awareness that these factors can also revert. The immersion into these factors takes place with an understanding of their impermanency, which in turn ceases the sprouting of arrogance too. When the factors of individual existence are non-favorable, an individual with a developed virtue of responsibility understands this as a test of one's virtues of courage, patience, equanimity, etc. The true depth of one's virtues is only known in unfavorable situations. This happens when one is aware that the present unfavorable situations are of one's own making. This makes one accept the present as a learning opportunity to understand the fallacies that lie within one's mental factors and the present situation as an opportunity to learn and overcome those vices. The individual then becomes aware of the present actions. The present actions are going to determine one's future conditions of existence. If there is a lack of awareness and understanding of the impermanency of the duties, one is still creating a bank of karmic conditions to experience in the future. And the cycle of karmic conditions never ceases. But with the virtue of responsibility comes true awareness and understanding of present actions. Also, the total dependency on the other individual to understand and navigate the present state of existence and present set of duties ceases.

This true understanding of responsibility gives rise to the pure state of a blameless mind. When one takes responsibility for all types of actions, whether mental, verbal, or physical, one is able to observe them in detail. But if the individual blames all actions, be they mental, physical, or verbal, on the second person, then there is no learning intended. For one to learn and overcome the conditionings of the mind, one has to be responsible for their existence. If one is responsible for one's own conditions, then can the individual work on them to simplify them? If there is an emotion of distancing from the conditionings of the mind, how can there be emancipation from them? The distance and the neglect make their appearance in the mental space again and again. This cycle of appearance and disappearance of the mental conditionings keeps repeating itself in a loop. For an individual on the path of emancipation from these mental conditionings, the thought of neglect and distancing from one's own conditionings never helps.

For the development of the monk-mind there should be virtues developed in the mind. In the process of developing virtues, the primary action is the recognition of one's vices and then understanding their workings. The understanding of the workings of the vices is itself enough to be free of their existence. The virtue of responsibility makes sure that one's awareness is present toward the vices.

In everyday life, the individual proceeds to accomplish the duties of one's self-affirmations by totally immersing themselves in them. Even if the part of the duty is not suited to the mentality of one, the individual takes up the challenge to convert that disliking attitude of the part of the duty into liking. This is where the skill of responsibility lies. The responsible mind makes one take up the responsibilities of their duties with love. With love toward the duties of the self—affirmations—rise expertise or a deep sense of knowledge toward the self—affirmations. This knowledge leads to humility. Humility toward existence is an opportunity to expand one's mental and physical horizons. With humility in the background, one can be emancipated totally from the workings of the conditioned mind. With freedom from the conditioned mind and monk-mind development, human mental existence expands into the realm of the universe.

This is the ultimate responsibility of human existence: to be free from the workings of the conditioned mind and to be one with the existence of the universe.

Practices and Insights

The virtues determine the quality of the Monk – Mind. For the development of virtues, one actually attains higher mental states. The virtues or factors discussed earlier come pre-installed in the human mental space. However, one who wishes to develop a serene and developed mental state has to excavate themselves from the depths of their existing mental conditions. Some of the virtues or factors may exist in the mental space due to the continuity of one's practice of the development of the virtues. For some, it may be the first attempt to understand the mind and the goal of existence. The understanding and tuning of the virtues may differ from person to person due to the karmic conditions. Understanding virtues is not meant by the knowledge gained by reading books or listening to sermons. Understanding is meant when one's true existence is conveyed by the manifestation of the virtues in the individual's mental space and is related to self-experience. There is unity in one's existence through the manifestation of virtues. The total immersion of the mental space in the ocean of virtues is meant by the understanding of virtues. Reading books and listening to sermons do help, but that knowledge is not true knowledge because reading and listening do not totally engrave virtues into one's existence. Reading and listening are only two feel-good factors that can show or describe a beautiful mental state. Just like the description of the beauty of the Pacific Ocean cannot be compared to the authentic experience of viewing the expanse of the ocean in reality. The description of the understanding of the monk-mind states is to provide one with a view or motivation toward the existence of higher mental states rather than the misconception of the fact that their virtual understanding is enough for their manifestation in real life. The manifestation of virtues in mental space is the real experience one needs to attain.

As discussed earlier, the manifestation of virtues for everyone depends on karmic conditions. The karmic conditions determine the ease with which the seeds of virtue sprout in each. The speed and time may differ individually, but the sprouting only happens when there is determination by the individual for the flowering of the seeds of virtue. The determination leads one to the practices and insights by which one can manifest virtues in one's habit patterns and character.

The true meaning of spiritual practices is to undertake them and gain insights. The fruit of these spiritual practices is the developed mind of virtues, or the monk-mind. The heaven one attains through these spiritual practices is no fantasy but a reality. Reality is rooted in clarity of mind, action, and speech. One carries one's own heaven wherever one travels. These are the practices and insights one has to understand. The existence of the practices and insights are just the tools for developing the monk-mind states, just a means to an end. The individual existence of these practices is of no meaning. Separating the development of virtues from practices and insights is a misconception one must avoid. There is a deep dependency of the factors of the monk's mind with the practices and insights. If the practices and insights do not result in the development of virtues, there should be an understanding that the aims of the practices and insights have not been understood completely. The isolation of spiritual practices and insights from reality has to be removed; rather, there should be an amalgamation with the reality of existence. The mastery of the practices and the understanding of insights are not based on the skill level of how well one excels in the spiritual practices but on the ease of the virtues one inculcates in the mental states. The main aim of these practices is to simplify and decondition the conditions of the mind.

Existence has provided the human realm with the tools it needs to navigate these mental states. The practices are meant for learning and being aware of the existence of these tools. At the same time, the practices also help in sharpening these tools inbuilt into human existence. At the same time, the insights act as a guidebook for the implementation of these tools on the objects. The objects in the realm of human existence are the conditions of the conditioned mind. Well, what are the tools that human existence is naturally endowed with? The tools are the body, breath, and mind. The body, breath, and mind are to be shaped and prepared in such a way that all past conditionings are removed and one becomes unified with the intention of existence for the individual. This is the perpetual aim of the monk—the mind or the development of virtues in the mental space. Just as an artisan creates a beautiful sculpture of stone by removing unwanted shapes and sizes of the rock, the individual, with the determination of developing the monk-mind, sculpts the mind off the conditionings with the help of tools such as the body, breath, and mind. The essentiality of the three is in their interdependency and extreme potency to remove and wade past the conditionings of the mind. The conditionings of the mind have stuck on due to habit patterns of unawareness.

These spiritual practices take into consideration the body, breath, and mind as a way to remove all the past conditionings and excavate the seeds of virtue that lie deep in the realm of human existence. The habit patterns of the conditioned mind are tough to remove as they are deeply engraved into the mind. The emotions of fear and anxiety become associated when one starts to tend to the mind. This new tendency to remove the habits of the conditioned mind requires a tremendous amount of determination and courage. Courage and determination are built by these spiritual practices of the body, breath, and mind to overcome fear and anxiety.

The tangible proof of one's existence is the presence of the body. The unification of the habit patterns of the body with awareness of the monk-mind is the aim of the spiritual practices. The breath is the proof of life in one. In the effort of the individual to align with existence, the most potent force one is endowed with is the breath. The spiritual practices are meant to align the breath in such a way that it provides a strong base for the virtue of awareness. The breath also controls the workings of the mind. The mind and the breath are strongly interconnected. For healthier states of mind, the wholesome habit patterns of the breath are to be cultivated. The main differentiator that separates human existence from other creations is the presence of a well-developed mind. The ability to think is what differentiates a human from animals and other non-living beings. The mind, which is not rooted in reality, but in some far-fetched fantasy of wants and expectations, has to be developed in a way to be aware of reality. The reality of impermanence and constant change. The description and essence of reality are true insights. Even though one is awake, the mind that wanders with the karmic conditions of the conditioned mind is rooted in a dreaming state. The insights help in providing a view of reality through awareness of the nature of existence. The nature of existence is to be reflected by the mind. This only happens when the dirt of the conditioned mind is removed. The initial aim of the insight is to be aware of the conditions one's life revolves around; when the conditions come into sight, then one can navigate through the abyss of the conditioned mind. This is true awakening, the awakening from the dream of the conditioned mind to the natural or monk-mind state.

For a sportsman to play the sport, he has to practice efficiently and ardently to excel. The sports player does the practices in such a way that, during a game, the individual is able to tackle all the opponent's tactics with ease. Similarly, the spiritual practices and insights are made to make the individual tackle the conditioned mind with ease. More with respect to understanding and developing the courage to face one's own anxieties and fears. When one practices to develop virtues, one becomes an expert in living life in the true sense.

Practices and Insights

1. Discipline

2. Relaxation

3. Concentration

4. Meditation

5. Awareness

6. Intention

7. Daily reflections

Discipline

When the word discipline is uttered, there is a fear that a set of rules is going to appear about a way of life. A set of dos and don'ts is going to appear in life. It is important to understand that the main aim of discipline is to be free of all conditions. It is meant to be free of fear and anxiety. The only freedom that comes with discipline is freedom through awareness. True freedom is freedom on the basis of awareness rather than just following the habit patterns of the conditioned mind. If discipline in life does not free one from the conditioned mind but, in response, creates an even greater mental block, the true essence of discipline is not understood. Of course, by inculcating discipline in life, there are going to be certain changes in lifestyle and way of thinking, but the existence of discipline is to be free from the workings of the conditioned mind, rather than taking a false pride in just following a certain set of rules in life. The rules that govern life are meant to free one from the existing shackles of the mind.

If the true meaning of discipline is freedom, then one could continue with the existing set of habit patterns and lifestyle. It is important to understand that the impressions of the conditioned mind are strong and that the individual cannot differentiate between wholesome and unwholesome states of mind. If one is just trying to pacify the habit patterns of the conditioned mind, there is no freedom from them. Discipline is the effort to break the cycle of the conditioned mind. Discipline overrides the impressions of the conditioned mind. This makes the individual observe the vicious cycle of expectations the conditioned mind puts one into. One clearly starts to understand that there is no true satisfaction and contentment in trying to fulfill the conditions of the mind, as the impressions of the mind become stronger with the effort of the individual to pacify the conditioned mind. Just as a pupil learning the piano from the maestro in the earlier stages of practice has to have a disciplined approach to learn the basic notes and keys of the piano, with time the disciple does not seem to view it as a burden as it has become a way of life for the individual. For a seeker on the path of the monk – mind one has to become a disciple of the existence or the natural state of mind to be free from the conditioned mind. With time and perseverance, when the pupil of the piano maestro becomes an expert, the seeker on the path of the monk-mind becomes an expert in understanding the natural or monk-mind way of life, which is based on the perfection of virtues.

In order to bring discipline into the way of thinking or just one's own existence, there need to be subtle changes in the way of life. Just as in the journey from the gross to the subtle, from the body to the mind, it is important to discipline the body first. Even before one starts to discipline the body, one has to discipline the individual lifestyle. The impressions of the mind get translated into lifestyle choices. The individual slowly and steadily needs to balance lifestyle habits in order to be able to understand and break away from the conditions of the mind. Lifestyle choices are reflections of one's state of mind. To abstain from adhering to the conditioned mind, these changes are necessary, and with these changes, slowly and steadily, one observes a change in mindset, which translates into confidence and perseverance on this noble path. Meanwhile, a change in lifestyle does not mean relinquishing daily duties and retiring into caves and mountain monasteries like the usual conception of a monk. These lifestyle changes are subtle changes that every individual, irrespective of their present situation, can follow. As discussed earlier, it is to translate the mindset of a true monk into the daily activities of human existence. By the word lifestyle, it is meant by the individual's daily essential activities. To bring awareness into the daily essential routine is the main aim of discipline. Secondly, monitor the physical aspect of the daily routine so that these activities become an exercise of awareness rather than a habit pattern of the conditioned mind. Discipline of lifestyle is meant by the food habits one enjoys, the rest one gives to oneself, and also by the daily hygiene routines one needs to tend to. These are as important as the isolated spiritual practices the individual focuses on. The isolated practices are meant by the practices of relaxation, concentration, and meditation. These are isolated practices, as the individual needs to be removed from undertaking the daily duties of life to attend to them. As the differentiation from these basic activities to the so-called spiritual practices causes a gap between reality and There is an intense interdependency between these isolated practices and the disciplined lifestyle in a way that they complement each other on the path of the monk-mind. It is important to observe the functions of daily routine as a spiritual practice and the isolated practices of spirituality as a part of daily routine. The conversion of each action into an exercise of awareness means the conversion of the daily routine into a spiritual practice. The awareness then eventually leads to knowledge of the conditioned mind. One becomes aware that all these basic actions were lacking a wholesome state of mind and were being done under the influence of the conditioned mind. This knowledge of the effect of the conditioned mind on the basic actions essential for existence makes one truly aware and alert. And then eventually leads to emancipation from the unwholesome habit patterns of the conditioned mind. This emancipation from the conditioned mind leads one to manifest one's existence in the natural state of mind. This natural state of mind is the monk-mind, which is based on the perfection of virtues. This is the core aim of bringing discipline into daily life routines.

Food Habits

The sensation of hunger is ever-present in all living beings. The feeling of hunger gets translated into eating habits. If hunger is not quenched, there is a feeling of discomfort. Food is intended to primarily quell the discomfort of hunger. The awareness of the utility of food is to be remembered at all times. The individual is under the influence of society, culture, climate, and habitat, and these factors affect one's food habits. Food habits mean the type of food one consumes, the portion of food one consumes, and the time periods during which one consumes food. These factors of culture, climate, and habitat are the result of one's karmic conditionings. When the effects of the karmic conditionings get blanketed by the conditioned mind, this results in a lack of awareness of the food we consume. The total idea of food habits and nutrition, with the effect of the conditioned mind, only gets confined to these factors. Awareness of food is the knowledge of the utility of the food one consumes. It is important to understand that every individual is born with a set of karmic conditions; however, what differentiates the individual from the rest is the awareness of the karmic conditionings with the help of the mind. To translate the awareness of karmic conditionings into daily life is to be aware of all the factors that are responsible for one's own existence. Food or eating habits are major factors that can create awareness of the individual's karmic conditionings, because without food, there is no life. There is a set idea of food that is determined by one's upbringing. This results in strong habit patterns of food and cuisine. In this cycle of habit patterns, one usually forgets the major role that food has to play in an individual's existence. The role that food and nutrition have to play is primarily to give nutrition to the body for a smooth experience of living and to quell the discomfort of hunger. The body is the supreme instrument that has been endowed with human existence by nature. Food not only acts as a fuel for this instrument, but it is also a medicine to overcome the hiccups that arise in it. Secondly, it is to quell the discomfort of the feeling of hunger. With the presence of a feeling of hunger, the mind only tends to the discomfort caused by it. With the concentration of the mind on the discomfort, it becomes arduous for the mind to develop into a virtuous state of existence. This is true awareness of food habits. With the effect of the conditioned mind, one thinks that the true nature of food is to please the habit of the perception of taste created by the conditioned mind. The individual then relates food to the perception of fixed taste textures, which are habituated to by the conditioned mind. And when the habituated tastes come into contact with the related sensual organs, then there arises a false perception of nutrition and comfort. With awareness of food and eating habits, one is in possession of the knowledge that the taste of the habituated food and cuisine has nothing to do with the true value of nutrition, which has to protect and take care of the body. The habituated taste is only due to the effects of society, culture, climate, and habitat. One just has to be aware of these factors. There is nothing wrong with consuming the food one is habituated to, but it is also important to be aware of the factors that have led one to become habituated to a certain type of food habit and cuisine. The practice of discipline in the way that an individual consumes food is to be free from the conditions of taste, cuisine, and eating habits. The discipline is to raise awareness that the main aim of food is to provide nutrition to the body and be free from hunger pains.

To discipline an individual's eating habits, one has to start consuming food without the conditions of taste. This does not mean that the food consumed should be bland, but the mindset with which one consumes food should be without any conditions of taste. The conditioned mind is always in search of a familiar taste and texture in food. The search for familiarity with habituated foods and cuisines in taste and texture should be avoided. Even if the food appeals to the taste buds, there is awareness of the quantity of food one consumes. Food is not an indulgence but only a major factor for a healthy body and mind.

Disciplining food habits is to remove the question of what one is consuming. And to ask, why is one consuming food? The answer lies in the fact that food is only meant to nourish the body, so that ailments can be fought over by the body by developing an excellent immune system and the physical structure of the body is well-maintained. To maintain a well-maintained physical structure, one must be free from obesity as well as being skinny. This healthy body provides a solid base for the mind to contemplate higher mental states; if not, then the mind gets stuck fixing ailments. For food to act as proper fuel for the individual's body, there should be a proper time distribution of when to consume food so that the body can digest the food evenly and that food does not become a load on the digestive system of the body. This is true disciplining of food habits in the physical sphere.

While consuming food, the individual should also be mentally prepared, as the mind has a direct effect on the digestive system. There should be total awareness while consuming food. The awareness that the food consumed is a gift of nature to protect and nurture the body and the mind so that the individual for the time period of existence lives a healthy life and the energy received from the consumption of food is used in the effort for attaining higher mental states of virtue. This mental state of gratitude toward food helps in converting the food into superfoods, just as awareness helps in converting the energy produced from food consumption into higher mental states of existence. The view that food is medicine for the body and its recovery rather than an indulgence for the taste buds is disciplining the food habits of the individual. At the same time, one also occasionally needs to let go and indulge in the food habits the mind craves, but only with the precaution that indulgence does not become a habit.

Sleep Cycle

Food helps protect and nourish the body. To maximize nourishment, the body and mind need rest. The rest for the body and mind is obtained through deep sleep. The understanding of sleep and rest is very important for the true development of the individual. For the individual to experience deep sleep, they should understand the three states of existence, i.e., the conscious, subconscious, and unconscious. The aim is not to go into detail about these three states. But an understanding of the potency of these states helps the individual use them for a better understanding of life.

The conscious state is the state of mind when one usually terms oneself as awake. In reality, the true conscious state of mind is the mind without the conditioned mind. There is a total acceptance of reality without the conditions of the mind. This is true awareness of the objects of the mind, without conditions.

The subconscious mind is the intermediary between the conscious and unconscious minds. One can understand it as a dreaming state, as there is awareness but not enough to relate it to reality. That is why there is no total comprehension of the events that have taken place in the mental realm.

The unconscious state is a state of nothingness. After the period of the unconscious state ends, one comes into the state of consciousness with the knowledge of nothingness, i.e., the individual returns with the experience of no knowledge of mental and physical objects.

This state of unconsciousness is the state where the body and mind get the maximum rest for recovery. Maximum recovery happens due to the lack of indulgence in the mental objects present in the mind. When there is no indulgence in the objects of the mind, the mind does not use the energy produced from the consumption of food to satisfy the conditions of the mind. The conditions of the mind translate the energy gained by the food into the physical working of the body and mental gymnastics. This needs to be avoided as it makes the individual plagued with fatigue. The energy saved from consumption by the mind is then used for recovery and rest. The discipline of the cycle of sleep is primarily to enter the state of unconsciousness with awareness. With awareness, the mind tends to take rest and recuperate so that it can work on itself to use the conserved energy to work on developing virtues rather than using it to satisfy the conditions of the mind.

This awareness is meant by disciplining the sleep cycle. The deep rest required for the body and the mind is meant by sleep. It is important to know that lack of sleep and excess sleep are both harmful. The notion that sleep is a waste of time or is a form of lethargy is a misconception. Sleep is essential for a healthy body and mind. At the same time, when an individual indulges in excessive sleep, they are adding fuel to the fire of unwholesome states of mind, as excessive sleep contributes to lethargy and dullness of the mind. The balance of the time period of sleep one manages during a lifetime is the discipline of the sleep cycle.

The need to discipline the sleep cycle is very important. The night is actually the time for the human realm to sleep and take rest. The entirety of existence takes rest at night. As the sun sets, the human monk-mind should actively discipline itself to enter a deep state of rest during this time. Humans are not nocturnal animals and this fact needs to be remembered. The cycle of day and night is to be replicated in the mental realm of human existence. The natural absence of light during the night provides a comfortable environment for the body and the mind to rest and be without any conditions. As the sun rises, so should the human mind rise from the state of the unconscious to the conscious. Due to the effect of the conditioned mind, there is an imbalance between these two states of existence. This imbalance sends mixed signals of rest and activity to the body and the mind. The imbalance between these two states leads to confusion in the mind, and then the mind is not able to send the proper signals to the body. When confusion arises in the signals, there is a miscommunication between the body and the mind. The mind does not understand the needs of the body, and the body is not able to convey its requirements to the mind. The miscommunication leads to stress and delusion. The stress and delusion of the mind then convert themselves into physical ailments of the body. Physical ailments are also caused by a lack of working in tandem between different body parts. This makes the synchronization between these two states very important. The mind and the body get the right signals to go to rest and to be awake at particular periods of time when there is discipline in the sleep cycle. This results in the well-oiled machinery of the body and the mind. Of course, due to external factors, there are going to be distractions in the cycles of rest and activity. The individual then makes a point to correct the course of the sleep cycle so that the synchronization is back in place.

The discipline of food and sleep cycles is majorly responsible for a balanced mind and body. With the presence of a balanced mind and body, an individual can put themselves on the track of the monk-mind.

Hygiene

There are two types of hygiene routines: mental hygiene and physical hygiene. Mental hygiene is maintained by developing virtues, or the monk-mind. In the meantime, the topic to be pondered here is physical hygiene. Physical hygiene plays an important role in day-to-day activities. For the development of the mind, the body acts as an instrument for the attainment of higher mental states. If the instrument endowed upon human existence by nature is not cared for and protected, then the path to higher mental states becomes difficult. If there is no physical body, then there is no basis for the mind. For the mind to function properly, it needs a sound body. Without a sound body, there can't be a sound mind. With the daily practice of physical hygiene, the body can be cared for and protected. By hygiene, it is not meant by using fragrant perfumes or expensive clothes. The purpose of understanding hygiene is to understand and be aware of the day-to-day bodily functions so that the instrument is kept in proper condition.

For the mind to be fresh and light, the stomach should be light and empty. The individual's cycle of ablution should be synchronized. One should attend nature's call within regular intervals of time. Keeping that in mind, the individual should plan out a suitable diet and water intake. With the production of energy from the consumption of food, there are toxins that get released into the body. These toxins need to be flushed out. The flushing out of the toxins takes place with the proper consumption of water. Water not only purifies the external physical body but also the internal body mechanisms. These functions of internal purification play an important role in the discipline of hygiene. The discipline of internal hygiene also plays an important role in regulating the sleep cycle, as a light stomach and toxin-free body help relax the body, which results in a synchronized working of the body and the mind. The proper discharge of toxins and fecal matter at regular intervals ensures that the body remains disease-free. With the body disease-free the mind develops the capability to focus on developing the mind in such a way that the mind becomes calm and easy.

With the discipline of external hygiene, the body from the outside is tended to. The body needs to be washed and made free of odor and dirt, as the basic step of awareness starts with the awareness of the body. A good wash of the body helps in rejuvenating the body. A daily habit of a full-body wash with water is very helpful. This rejuvenation makes the body relaxed, which in turn helps the individual be aware of the entirety of the body. The mind can feel settled for the practices and be ready to take on the objects that arise in the mental realm. This is the discipline of the hygiene of the external physical body.

Abstinence

The discipline of abstinence is often misunderstood by the individual. It is seen as a spoilsport. If only there was no abstinence, life would have been easy. The main intention of abstinence is to actually make life easier rather than complicate things in life. The habit patterns of the conditioned mind make it difficult for the individual to view the true intention of the practice of abstinence. Abstinence is usually seen as a negation of life, but in reality, abstinence is the negation of the workings of the conditioned mind. The habit patterns of the conditioned mind are so strong that the true essence of life can be viewed by following those patterns. This makes it difficult for the individual to rise above the conventional meaning of abstinence and delve into the true meaning of the practice of abstinence. When there is excessiveness involved in behavior and action, it signifies the role of the conditioned mind. Be it excessiveness of plenty or excessiveness of insignificance, both of these are to be reflected upon. The practice of discipline, where the excessiveness of both ends of the spectrum is looked down upon, is meant by abstinence from the working of the conditioned mind. The habit patterns of this excessiveness are to be evolved through the true practice of the discipline of abstinence. Through moderation in lifestyle and habit patterns, one can overcome the strong effects of the habit patterns of the conditioned mind, which are excessive. The discipline of moderation in all aspects of life is meant by abstinence. This discipline of abstinence from the conditioned mind brings balance into day-to-day lifestyle patterns, be it food habits, sleep cycles, or the practice of hygiene.

The balance of mental states takes place when one understands that abstinence is moderate indulgence. The usual concept of abstinence is seen as a negation of indulgence. The negation of indulgence in food habits, sleep cycles, and the practice of hygiene. In practice, abstinence should necessarily be seen as the practice of indulgence in moderation in the aforementioned daily life activities. The practice of abstinence thus gets translated into abstinence from excessive indulgence in opulence and, at the same time, penance, which is related to negation.

With this right view on the practice of discipline in indulgence, there arises an awareness of the nature of existence. The nature of existence is impermanence. This nature of impermanence can be seen and viewed with this discipline of abstinence. If one is too engrossed in the far-end spectrums of excessiveness, it becomes difficult to contemplate the true nature of impermanence. With the practice of moderation in daily life, which is the essence of abstinence, one can be able to accept life in its true nature. With moderation, the individual can experience the essence of the objects existence has to offer and, at the same time, reject the same objects when the need arises to be free of them.

With an understanding of abstinence, one should apply it to the actions of daily life. The most important factor gets translated into food and drinking habits. The habit of moderation leads to abstinence from indulging in intoxicants. The main purpose of the practices and insights is to enter a virtuous state of mind. The virtuous state of mind is also the natural state of mind. With the indulgence of the individual in intoxicants, the mind loses its awareness, and the individual forgets one's state of being. This slowly leads the conditions of the mind to take control over the individual. This has to be prevented. The prevention, though, does not have to be forced; rather, it should be a natural process; the natural transition only happens with understanding and effort. Understanding abstinence with the right effort can lead to healthy food and drinking habits. The consumption of intoxicants never takes long to form a habit. This habit of consumption results in deterioration of the mind and the body. The deterioration of the mind and the body can never serve the purpose of fulfilling the aim of achieving the monk-mind. The use of intoxicants in any form except when prescribed by a physician makes the effect of the conditioned mind on the individual strong. It is very important that the individual striving to attain higher states forgo with one's own will these deluding habits. One needs to experience true happiness, that is, happiness from experiences like being kind, courageous, patient, etc., rather than falling into the trap of the temporary happiness that the intoxicants have to offer.

It is also important to understand another law of existence, which is that the mind is developed based on the type of food habits an individual practices. For the practice of developing the monk's mind, it is important that the mind be flexible and malleable to understand the true motive of one's own existence and the nature of the objects that existence brings up in the mental realm. The consumption of intoxicants makes the mind heavy and dull, which in turn makes the path of the monk-mind difficult to travel on. The seeker on the path of the monk—the mind—has to be alert and aware of the food habits one practices, as the food consumed plays an important and direct role in the formation of the mind and the body.

For the understanding and practice of discipline, abstinence plays an important part. With the practice of abstinence, does one truly overcome the habit patterns of the conditioned mind? To overcome the habit patterns of the conditioned mind is not an easy task, for each and every action of human existence must be transformed. The first step of discipline, with the right understanding, plays an important role. When the individual starts practicing the discipline of daily essential actions, there is a shift in mental tendencies. The shift in mental tendencies then makes the individual believe in the virtues of courage and patience. The practice of discipline in life makes one move closer toward the development of courage, virtue, and patience in life. The sprouting of courage and patience leads to faith in one's own disciplined lifestyle. This, in turn, makes discipline a natural way of life rather than an imposed one. The basis of all virtues is courage and patience, and the basis of the virtues of courage and patience is the practice of discipline.

Relaxation

The practice of relaxation needs to be understood and brought into action to undertake practices with insights. The human mind, due to external factors and the effect of the conditioned mind, becomes engaged in a race against time. The race against time becomes so intense that one forgets to live life the way existence intends it to be lived. The law of nature is contraction and expansion. While nature is in an expansive phase, the mind needs to engage in the duties of self-affirmation. At the same time, during the phase of contraction, there should be relaxation of the mind, body, and breath. This is where relaxation acts as a foundation for introspection and meditation on the objects of the mind. While engaging in the duties of the self-affirmations, it becomes easy due to the effect of the conditioned mind to only get immersed in the duties and actions of the self-affirmations. This forms a habit of goal-setting in the mind. The habit of goal-setting against the will of time causes tension and delusion. The only way to resolve this mindset is to understand and practice relaxation. When one gets relaxed, the race for the completion of the duties of self-affirmation also slows down. This releases unnecessary tensions in the body, mind, and breath. It is not totally frowned upon to set goals and aspirations required for the self—affirmations. But the view is to be realistic in setting the goals and aspirations required for the completion of the present self-affirmation. Such goal-setting based on reality only happens when one practices relaxation and understanding. Relaxation is not aimless wandering of the body and the mind but a state of awareness of being apart from the duties and aspirations of the goals of the self—affirmations. Apart from the race of these aspirations, there is tranquility in the culmination of the tension in the mind and the body. The presence of tension in the mind is the result of the presence of the conditioned quality of expectation in the mind. The effect of the conditioned mind then directly affects the workings of the body and the breath. Relieving the body, mind, and breath from the expectations of the conditioned mind helps release tension and brings in a sense of calmness. This presence of calmness gets transformed into a relaxed state of being.

Relaxation of the Body

The body is proof of the gross existence of the individual. The involvement of the individual in fulfilling the goals of the self—affirmations— happens primarily through the instrument of the body. As discussed earlier, food and sleep habits help maintain physical balance. The practice of relaxation is meant to be understood and practiced during the conscious state. When one attempts to relax the body, the signal sent to the brain is to fall asleep, but the training here is to be relaxed in the state of awareness. Even though a suitable amount of sleep is important for relaxing the body, it is also important to relax the body in awareness of the conscious, as day-to-day actions happen in the state of consciousness. Usually, when an individual attempts to relax, their mental state slips into an unconscious state. This happens due to the habit patterns of the conditioned mind. The conditioned mind directs the mind as a habit to fall into sleep just as the awareness of relaxation starts taking place. In the initial stages of practicing relaxation with awareness, the individual has to fight this habit of falling asleep. The difference between falling asleep and being relaxed in awareness is that when sleep takes over, there is no presence of mental awareness. But while relaxing the body in an awakened state, there is a presence of awareness. The presence of awareness plays an important role in differentiating between the workings of the conditioned mind and the natural state of mind, which is the monk-mind.

The book does not present itself as a guidebook on the practice of relaxation; however, an attempt at understanding the basics of relaxation can surely be made. To start with, the individual needs to cool down the body by having a wash or washing the limbs with water that is comfortable for the body. One should put on some loose-fitting clothes with mild color patterns. The practice could be done either lying down or while sitting in a comfortable posture. For beginners, the posture for relaxation while lying down should be avoided, as the habit patterns of the conditioned mind make the individual fall into a sleeping state. It is important to understand that awareness while being awake is practiced. While sitting down, the posture needs to be comfortable for the individual, and at the same time, it needs to be ensured that the body, neck, and spine are perpendicular to the ground. This posture can also be practiced while sitting on a chair. With awareness and slow movements, the eyes can be closed. With the eyes closed, one should be aware that there is no tension on the shoulders. If the shoulders are stressed or pulled, make sure to put them back down in the resting position. Awareness can slowly be brought to the toes of the feet. One can feel with the eyes closed the toes and feel if there is any tension, then slowly move upwards to feel the ankle, the shin, the knees, the thighs, and so on and so forth in sequence to the head. With awareness, the person can feel tension in the body part that is in focus. If there is any feeling of tightness or tension, one only needs to be aware of it. When one becomes aware of any tightness or a feeling of tension, that awareness itself helps in releasing the body from the tension and tightness. This process needs to be followed from the toes to the head and from the head to the toes with total awareness. The same should be followed in both cases of awareness, i.e., from top to bottom and bottom to top. This practice needs to be repeated three to five times in a sitting. It is important to notice that in the early stages of practice, it is easy for the practitioner to go to sleep, but with the help of awareness and due practice, the awareness remains with a relaxed and calming effect on the body.

Relaxation of breath

With the immersion of the individual in the duties of the self—affirmations—one forgets that one is also a breathing being. With a lack of awareness, the usual rhythm of inhalation and exhalation of the breath becomes distorted. The natural breath flow becomes artificial in nature. Artificial in the sense that there is forced inhalation and exhalation. This artificial breathing habit is also a major factor in producing illness. The breathing patterns act as a bridge between the body and the mind. If the breath is relaxed, then the mind and body also follow suit. For some, relaxing the breath at the start of practice can be a difficult task. Those individuals can start by relaxing the body and slowly start relaxing the breath. The breath and the mind are two sides of the coin. If one starts to relax the breath, then the mind also becomes quiet. And the same happens when the mind becomes quiet, just as the breath flow becomes natural. Breath is the most potent weapon an individual is endowed with. The flow of the natural breath is the way to the natural state of mind, or the monk-mind.

The prerequisites for the overview of the practice of relaxation for the breath are the same as for the relaxation of the body. One can also practice relaxation of the breath while lying down on the back as well as in a sitting posture. For beginners, it is advised to practice sitting posture to avoid the habit of falling asleep. Take a deep inhalation. It is important to note that inhalation is total nasal inhalation; the mouth is not to be used. Here, the habit pattern of diaphragmatic breathing needs to be cultivated. The inhalation is to be started without any force, and the inhalation should take the maximum amount of time, i.e., the maximum capacity of the lungs should be filled with air. After the completion of inhalation, exhalation should also be practiced through the nasal passage. The process of exhalation should also be practiced in a slow and gentle manner. During exhalation, it is also important that all the air in the lungs is thrown out. This relaxation should be practiced for three to five cycles. One cycle is the complete process of inhalation and exhalation.

Relaxation of the Mind

The most strenuous part of the practice of relaxation is relaxation of the mind. The nature of the mind is that of a monkey. It never stays still and is always in search of some object to hold on to. The mind is always in search of some object to hold on to because of the habit patterns, which are to worry and think about situations and experiences. To culminate this habit, the practice of relaxation of the mind is a must. The basis of stress is in the mind because of this worrying attitude of the mind. This attitude creates stress and distorts the natural breathing pattern; the distorted breathing pattern becomes a root cause of ailments in the physical body. The cycle of causes and their actions starts with the habit patterns of the mind, which get translated into the breath and the body. That is a reason why the mind needs to stay relaxed and in a wholesome state; if it does not, then the balance of life gets distorted. A calm mind can only guide the individual to the natural state of mind, which is the monk-mind state.

The pre-requisites for the overview of the practice of relaxation for the mind are the same as for the relaxation of the body and the breath. For the mind to be calm and relaxed, the practice of relaxation should be practiced in a sitting posture only. The sitting posture obviously should be comfortable. When one feels agitated and in an uneasy state of mind, it is important to let go of all duties and actions for a while and just sit down without any care of the world. With the eyes closed, let there be a conversation with the mind. The conversation with the mind to let go. The mind should come to know that the individual is not going to abruptly stop the flow of thoughts that are taking place in the present. All the feelings and emotions that are arising in the mind that are going to be played and which are being played in the present in the mental realm will not have any interference by the individual. The individual is only going to observe the happenings in the mind and let them play till the end. There is no time limit set here by the individual for this practice. As the observance of the feelings goes on, the mind becomes exhausted, and the rising of feelings and emotions comes to a halt. Suddenly, one can experience a deep calmness in the mental realm; this calmness then translates into relaxation of the mind.

The practice of all three types of relaxation—mental, physical, and breath—forms a strong foundation for the further practice of concentration and daily life meditations. Another important factor in the practice of relaxation is inculcating discipline with it. Discipline in the sense that the practice of relaxation is done regularly. Regularity is maintained when the mind takes up the determination of following the practice for a certain period of time regularly. During this fixed period of time, the individual has to ensure that the regularity of the practice is maintained. Regularity means that one practices at a fixed, determined time of the day. The preferred time is morning, as the individual is fresh and agile because of the rest they have experienced during sleep. After the practice during the determined period, one can reflect on the effects that the practices have had on the individual. The effects can be favorable or unfavorable, but the intention is to pivot the energies of human mentality to understand the practices at a deeper level. With this new understanding, one can again take up a new determination of a time period to practice with this new knowledge based on the experience of practice. This cycle of regularity in practice with determination and pivoting the new practice in accordance with individual experience is essentially the inclusion of discipline in the practice.

It is important to understand that the practice of relaxation helps regulate the basic functions of life. With the regulation of these functions, one remains disease-free mentally as well as physically. This helps the mind, body, and breath focus on climbing to higher mental states through the process of evolution. In the process of evolution, the conservation of all three types of energies, be they physical, mental, or praanic (the energy of divine breath), is of utmost importance. The practice of relaxation makes it possible for the individual to conserve these three types of energies. With this conservation of energies, can one use them for developing higher mental states through concentration and meditation?

This conservation of energy can lead to the direct development of the virtue of patience. With relaxation, the mind becomes calm and quiet. With this calm and quiet mind, the individual can process all the knowledge and respond to it rather than reacting to it. As discussed earlier, reaction is a habit pattern of the conditioned mind, whereas response is the action arising naturally from the natural or monk-mind space. For the seeker intending to practice in isolation from daily activities, the practice of relaxation is of significance, as relaxation helps the seeker accept the mental factors that arise during concentration and meditation. With a strong base of relaxation, the seeker or practitioner can move into the secondary stages of practice without any fear. The individual develops a strong sense of contentment with one's own sphere of existence. In simple words, the art of relaxation is to be free and just let go.

Concentration

The mind never sticks to a place, as it is always jumping from one object to another. This jumping habit of the mind is the habit of the conditioned or untrained mind. This habit pattern needs to be perfected with the practice of concentration. The practice of concentration helps the mind stick to a certain object for a fixed period of time without any interference from other mental factors. With the development of the practice of relaxation, the practice of concentration becomes adaptable to daily spiritual practices. It is important to understand that a concentrated mind does not only facilitate the journey on the path of the monk-mind but also facilitates having a balance in daily life situations. With the practice of relaxation, the mind becomes free and agile, and with this agility, the practice of concentration makes the mind sharp and focused. A sharp and focused mind with the agility and freedom of relaxation is being trained by the individual.

The monk-mind state is a state of constant awareness. For awareness to sustain itself, it should have the power of concentration. For the sustenance of concentration, the practice of awareness brings quality to the concentration. It is important to understand that awareness and concentration go hand in hand. The insight of awareness will be discussed in the chapters ahead, while understanding the insight of awareness is powered by the practice of concentration. Concentration and awareness are two sides of the same coin. For one to go deep into concentration, one has to be aware. Awareness slowly and steadily leads to a sharp, pointed mind. The awareness of a single mental or physical object for a fixed period of time without the hindrance of the habit patterns of the conditioned mind is called concentration. The object of awareness is to be chosen appropriately by the individual to go deep into concentration. The object of awareness must not be an object that is resultant of the habit pattern of the conditioned mind. The object of the mind should be a wholesome object. The definition of a wholesome object is one that is free from the conditions of the mind. The object of the mind should exist in reality and must have the true characteristics of nature embedded in it. When the practice of relaxation is practiced, the chaos of the mind is subdued. With the subdued chaos, the individual can choose a wholesome object according to their karmic conditionings. With this awareness, attention rises toward the object, and as the time of attention elongates, the depth of concentration also increases. The step-by-step process toward training the mind to become sharp and alert with the practice of constant awareness of wholesome objects and to be free from the strong habit patterns of the conditioned mind is the true fruition and aim of the practice of concentration.

To develop concentration, there are three objects of reference: the body, mind, and breath. Of the three, the concentration on the breath is the most effective. However, the overview of practice will be done from the gross to the subtle, i.e., from the object of the body to the object of the mind. Even though the object of breath is the most effective, it is not meant for everyone. One needs to know one's own nature and choose a suitable object for the mind according to one's own karmic conditioning.

Concentration on Body Parts

The body is the grossest proof of an individual's existence. The body needs to be seen as an instrument provided by existence for developing the monk-mind. The presence of the human body is proof of the natural existence of the individual. The parts of the body can be taken as wholesome objects for the development of the practice of concentration.

With this awareness, the individual, according to the individual's karmic conditionings, can choose a body part as an object for concentration and, with awareness, slowly develop the practice. The practice of concentration is to develop pure awareness without any chatter in the mind. The awareness of the chosen body part is meant by the awareness of the sensation that is occurring in the chosen part of the body. The feelings arising from the sensation must be observed without any conditions of good or bad, pleasant or unpleasant, and so on and so forth. There only needs to be constant observance of the sensations that occur on the chosen body part. At the same time, one needs to ensure that the constant commentary by the mind on the feelings of the sensation ceases. There should not be any utterance of the process of observation; for example, this sensation is neither good nor bad. Awareness is pure observance of the happenings without any filtration of any conditions. There is total silence, and the act of constant observation is only taking place.

The individual needs to cool down the body by having a wash or washing the limbs with water that is comfortable for the body. One should put on some loose-fitting clothes with mild color patterns. The practice could be done while sitting in a comfortable posture. While sitting down, the posture needs to be comfortable for the individual, and at the same time, it needs to be ensured that the body, neck, and spine are perpendicular to the ground. This posture can also be practiced while sitting on a chair. Slowly get into the practice of relaxation. After the practice of relaxation, one is ready to practice concentration. Choose a favorable body part that makes the mind aware and attentive without any exertion. The body parts belonging to the face are usually strong points of awareness. The points may be the center between the two eyebrow lines, the tip of the nose, or the center of the upper lip. These are usually very sensitive points that help the individual become aware of them. For some individuals, it can be the topmost part of the skull, the starting point of the upper spine, and also the center of the chest. These points of reference may differ from person to person due to different karmic conditions. One can practice being aware with total observance of the sensations on these body parts, which slowly helps in developing concentration. One can slowly and steadily indulge deeply in the practice by increasing the time from five minutes to one hour according to the individual's mental capacity without much exertion.

This is the practice of concentration with the help of awareness of the body parts.

Concentration with Breath

As discussed earlier, the most potent object for the mind is the breath. The breath is the bridge between the body and the mind. If one concentrates on the breath, then automatically the mind and body follow the flow of the breath. The breath is the most natural object that human existence is in possession of. There are no artificial factors associated with the flow of breath. Its significance is such that the presence of the flow of breath in the individual ensures that the individual is really alive. The breath is like a thread that connects the individual existence to the total existence as a whole. With the concentration on the object of the breath, the body and the mind of the individual get connected to the will of existence. When the body, mind, and breath get connected to their natural existence, it gives rise to the natural state of mind, or the monk-mind. This happens as the natural flow of breath controls the workings of the mind to flow in the direction of the sense organs. When awareness of the breath arises, the awareness guides the mind away from the interactions of the sense organs with the outside world. This interaction of the breath and the mind brings a sense of balance to all the spheres of existence, i.e., the mental, praanic, and physical. That is why the breath is the most potent object of awareness for the mind, as it can directly lead to the natural state without much contemplation. The individual needs to be aware of the fact that the object of concentration may differ from individual to individual due to karmic conditioning. Even though the object of breath is potent, one must understand and adapt to it according to one's interests and capabilities.

The individual needs to be aware of the natural exhalations and the inhalations that take place. When the cycle of exhalations and inhalations takes place, one needs to only observe the inhalation and exhalation, without any mental commentary. The aim is to be justly aware of the natural flow of breath without bringing in the commentary of the mind. The awareness of the natural flow of breath with mental silence for a specific period of time is meant by the concentration of mind with the breath.

The individual needs to cool down the body by having a wash or washing the limbs with water that is comfortable for the body. One should put on some loose-fitting clothes with mild color patterns. The practice could be done while sitting in a comfortable posture. While sitting down, the posture needs to be comfortable for the individual, and at the same time, it needs to be ensured that the body, neck, and spine are perpendicular to the ground. This posture can also be practiced while sitting on a chair. Slowly get into the practice of relaxation. After the practice of relaxation, one is ready to practice concentration. One needs to bring in awareness just inside the nose. Feel the sensation of the length of the in-breath and the sensation of the length of the out-breath. One needs to be aware of the change in time duration that takes place during the process of inhalation and exhalation. Slowly and steadily, one will be able to observe the minute changes in-breath patterns. If one is not able to feel the sensation of the in-breath and the out-breath in the nasal area, one can be aware of the movement of the stomach during the breathing process. One can practice being aware with total observance of the sensations on the breath, which slowly helps in developing concentration. One can slowly and steadily indulge deeply in the practice by increasing the time from five minutes to one hour according to the individual's mental capacity without much exertion.

This is the practice of concentration with the help of awareness of the breath.

Concentration with a Mental Object

The mind is a storehouse of impressions of past and present actions and experiences. Some of the impressions are an effect of the conditioned mind, while others are of the natural mind state or the monk-mind. The constant awareness of the mental factors of the natural state of the mind results in concentration in the mind. Concentration with the mind is a tricky path to walk, as the individual may struggle to differentiate between the mental factors of the conditioned mind and the natural mind. The mental object can be any wholesome object that is related to the experience of reality. One only needs to be aware of the mental impressions of reality. This awareness can be maintained through the practice of pure observance. It is important that the observance happen in a silent mind state, where there is no mental commentary on the present state of awareness or any intrusion from the conditions of the mind.

The individual needs to cool down the body by having a wash or washing the limbs with water that is comfortable for the body. One should put on some loose-fitting clothes with mild color patterns. The practice could be done while sitting in a comfortable posture. While sitting down, the posture needs to be comfortable for the individual, and at the same time, it needs to be ensured that the body, neck, and spine are perpendicular to the ground. This posture can also be practiced while sitting on a chair. Slowly get into the practice of relaxation. After the practice of relaxation, one is ready to practice concentration. Practice with awareness of the mental factors is done by using the remembrance of the impressions of the experiences of the natural mind. The impression of nothingness can be used as the object of awareness. For the practice of nothingness, one must remember the sensation one wakes up to after deep sleep, i.e., "I enjoyed my sleep, yet I don't remember anything." This is the feeling of nothingness; one can remember a soothing experience of joy or contentment one has experienced and be aware of that sensation. One can be aware of the impressions of existence that affect the mind. The effects of coming into contact with a large water body, a beautiful mountain, or the vast expanse of the blue sky. It is important to remember that all the objects and the impressions should represent the nature of existence, and the impressions should belong to the natural state of mind. One can practice being aware with total observance of the sensations in the mental factors, which slowly helps in developing concentration. One can slowly and steadily indulge deeply in the practice by increasing the time from five minutes to one hour according to the individual's mental capacity without much exertion.

This is the practice of concentration with the help of awareness of mental factors.

It is important to understand that the aforementioned practices are just an overview. It is important to undertake these practices when a person is actually practicing them in their daily life. A proper guidance under a teacher is necessary.

With the practice of concentration, one can gain a certain level of mastery over the practice. The practice becomes effective by inculcating a certain level of discipline into it. The discipline of time. If the individual practices concentration at a certain time daily, the entire universe is ready to empower the individual with the power and energy required for understanding and expanding the horizons of the practice. The practice of concentration is not only helpful for the development of the monk's mind but also for gaining a certain level of mastery over the duties of daily life. Therefore, understanding the workings of the practice of concentration is important to the workings of the outer world as well as the workings of the inner world. This happens as concentration trains the mind to develop a faculty where the object, be it physical, mental, or psychic, can remain for a long time without any disturbance. When these objects remain for a long time without any disturbance, it helps the individual understand the workings of the object easily in a short amount of time. Which makes life easy and full of purpose to deal with.

Mastery over the practice of concentration can be very fascinating, but the individual should remember that it is just a means to an end. If one sharpens a knife and does not cut fruit with it, then the sharpening is of no use. Concentration only sharpens the faculties of the mind, body, and breath. These sharpened facilities need to be used to break or cut the conditions of the mind. The individual must be aware of this fact. With mastery over the practice of concentration, it leads to the mind being steady and still. When the mind becomes steady and still for a long time, a feeling of happiness and joy erupts. The joy and happiness are very intoxicating. One can start getting immersed in the joy of intoxication. One might find that this feeling of joy and happiness is the true nature of the monk-mind. With the practice of concentration, the other mental factors, which the individual is not habituated to, take a back seat. Only the factor of awareness remains. There becomes a union of the mental factor and awareness; this unity is the cause of happiness and joy. But the state of happiness and joy only remains until the individual's concentration; once the individual is out of the practice of concentration, all the unhabituated mental factors rise up, and the tranquility that was achieved during the practice also vanishes with due time. This happens due to the inability to develop the mind to use concentration appropriately. The individual needs to be aware of the use of concentration. The true nature of the mind is to maintain a perpetual state of tranquility rather than a temporary, good state of mind.

With the help of concentration, one can be attentive to the conditions and the mental factors for a long period of time. When this happens, the individual can truly understand the nature of the conditions of the mind. When one understands the nature of the conditions of the mind, one can meditate on their true state of existence. This is where the practice of concentration helps a lot. Also, the practice of concentration helps the mind develop immunity from the nature of the mind, which is to constantly move from one object to another. This constant movement from one mental object to another without any awareness is the habit of the conditioned mind, which is slowly being broken down by the practice of concentration. This helps in nurturing the mind into higher states of existence. By training the mind in the practice of concentration, the individual can slowly develop the virtues of courage, patience, and equanimity. With the development of concentration, the higher virtue of equanimity becomes more and more visible.

Meditation

The practice of discipline and relaxation is predominantly to purify the habit patterns of the mind; the practice of concentration is predominantly to purify the habit patterns of the breath. Meditation with awareness purifies the habit pattern of the mind. Subtler, the object of purification, becomes arduous in the practice of purification. The objects of the mind effect the existence of the individual on all the planes of existence, that is, the mental, physical, and praanic. The purification of the instrument of the mind helps to purify the body and the breath. The changes in the subtlest form of existence convert into drastic changes in the gross form of existence. The purification of the mind translates into the subsequent purification of the breath and the body.

The conditions of the mind get translated into habit patterns of the breath, the body, and the mind. With the presence of the habit patterns of the conditions in the mind, body, and breath, the individual can never return to the natural state of mind or the monk-mind state. The presence of the conditions results in creating a never-ending circle of karmic conditions, whether they are good or bad to experience. For the conditions to cease, one has to convert them into the natural state of mind. It is important to understand that ceasing the conditions of the mind is not meant literally. Total elimination or wiping out of the conditions is not possible in the physical aspect, but the true meaning of ceasing or eliminating the conditions is to slowly and steadily eliminate their effects on the workings of the mind. When the mind develops such immunity in a way that the conditions of the mind start losing their potency, then one starts to eliminate the presence of the conditions in the mind. The practice of meditation helps in overcoming the blossoming of the seeds of conditions while making the conditions non-existent to the individual. The purification of the mind from the conditions of the mind happens in the practice of meditation. This purification then translates into the habit patterns of the breath and the body. The purification of the breath and the body is meant by the removal of unconscious habit patterns.

To develop the capability of removing the conditions of the mind is to develop the wisdom by which the effects of the conditions can be terminated in their entirety. Developing the appropriate knowledge base through experience of awareness and contemplation of awareness leads to the development of the factor of wisdom. With the development of wisdom, one can analyze and see clearly the effects of the conditions of the mind and analyze the conditions in relation to the true nature of existence. This development of wisdom then makes the individual see past the effects of the conditioned mind and use the mental facilities to develop, through awareness and patience, the monk-mind qualities or virtues. These virtues are the true testament to human existence.

With the practice of wisdom, one is able to fine-tune the conditions of the mind. The development of wisdom to terminate the effects of the conditioned mind is the true practice of meditation. How does one overcome the effects of the conditioned mind? The first step in understanding the workings of the conditioned mind is to accept its existence. The human mentality is such that one tends to portray only the righteous virtues of the individual; even though the existence of righteousness in one is a reality, it need not be portrayed artificially. The individual has to accept the conditionings of the mind as a result of one's own actions rather than blaming their existence on the second person or on destiny. For an automobile mechanic to repair a fault in the car, he has to accept the presence of a fault in the mechanics of the car, then he can analyze the fault and rectify it. If the mechanic portrays the parts that work perfectly, then the fault will never be rectified. The fault in the car will remain unresolved because of the mechanic's obstructed view of accepting the totality of the car, which is a combination of faults and perfections. The mechanic does not need to rectify the perfectly working parts of the car but has the job only to fix the fault or the problem. It is the duty of the mechanic to accept and address the fault or problem in the car to fulfill the assigned job of being a mechanic. Human existence is also a mixture of virtues and factors of the conditioned mind. Just as the mechanic addresses the fault or the problem in the car, the individual is the mechanic of the mind, and to rectify the workings of the conditioned mind is the individual's duty. The rectification can only happen when the individual can see and accept the presence of the conditions in the mental sphere of existence. With awareness of the existence of mental conditionings, one can relate to them and find a way to overcome them. The only difference with the example of the car mechanic is that the fault in the car was caused by the handling of the owner of the car, whereas the conditions of the mind are caused by the individual's own actions. Only the mere acceptance of the presence of the conditioned mind is not sufficient to overcome their effects on human existence, but the acceptance of the conditions should be in its entirety, that the conditions exist and the root cause of the existence of the conditions are the actions of the individual, and no external factor has any role in it. This acceptance in the totality of the conditions helps in creating a mentality of total responsibility; this responsibility then creates a space for the rectification or transformation of the conditions into virtues, or the monk-mind state. By accepting the conditions, one might understand it as a form of self-condemnation. It is not self-condemnation but a form of self-love where one accepts the existence of oneself in its entirety.

With the acceptance of the conditions in the mental space, it leads to responsibility. Responsibility to undertake an action to transform the mental conditionings into virtues. The responsibility makes one observe the conditionings of the mind in reality rather than making the practice of meditation delve into mythical restorations of the mind. Often, the mind gets too involved in the mythical and supernormal experiences during the practice; even though the experience is fascinating, the factor of responsibility drags the mind down to reality and confronts the conditions of the mind. It is the responsibility of the individual to transform the conditions of the mind into virtues; this is the major duty that existence has endowed upon the human race.

For the mind to accept the conditionings, it is not easy and often does not come naturally to the mind. The mind needs to be trained in such a way that the individual accepts the conditions of the mind and transforms them into virtues. This training is the meditation the monks or ascetics practice in deep forests and mountain monasteries. Just as one experiences pain when one inserts the whole-body part into hot water, the individual also experiences anxiety and fear when the individual confronts the conditions of the mind in totality. To be comfortable with the temperature of the water, the individual slowly and steadily makes sure that each and every body part has become accustomed to the temperature and then immerses the whole-body part into hot water. The pain experienced is minimal. The practice of meditation is to habituate the mind with the presence of the conditions. This habit of awareness of the presence of the conditions in the mental space makes the mind well equipped to solve the knots and barriers set up by these conditions. This habit of awareness makes the mind well equipped to handle the fear and anxiety created when the factors of the conditioned mind arise. The mind can analyze the conditions and find out the root cause of their existence. With knowledge of the genesis of the conditions, one is able to relate the existence of the conditions to the root cause. When the individual is completely able to relate to and observe the chain of events that unfold due to the rising or presence of the root cause, then the mind becomes alert and aware of the root cause and tries to distance itself from it. When the mind starts to slowly and steadily distance itself from the cause of the conditions of the mind, the cycle of manifestation and termination of the fruition of these conditionings comes to a complete halt. With the termination of the fruition of the conditionings, the virtues existing in the human sphere start to rise and bloom.

One can meditate on the conditions of the mind, breath, and body to overcome the conditionings. The root cause of the conditionings that translate into the body and the breath is the conditionings present in the mind. The meditation will be considered with respect to the conditioning of the mind.

The practice of concentration plays an important part in analyzing the workings of the conditioned mind. Concentration makes sure that the object for analysis remains in the mind for a long period of time. The usual habit of the mind is to jump from one object to another without any synchronization. The practice of concentration trains the mind to be still and focused on one single object at a time with full attention and awareness. With the practice of concentration, the individual is able to focus on the workings of the conditions for a long time and see the futility of their existence. With the mental silence created by concentration, the individual is able to see distinctively the effects and causes of the conditions present in the mental space. With this understanding, one needs to enter into the practice of meditation.

Meditation on mental conditionings

The individual needs to cool down the body by having a wash or washing the limbs with water that is comfortable for the body. One should put on some loose-fitting clothes with mild color patterns. The practice could be done while sitting in a comfortable posture. While sitting down, the posture needs to be comfortable for the individual, and at the same time, it needs to be ensured that the body, neck, and spine are perpendicular to the ground. This posture can also be practiced while sitting on a chair. Slowly get into the practice of relaxation. After the practice of relaxation, one needs to practice concentration. After one feels considerably absorbed into the practice of concentration, one needs to let go of the object of concentration. The individual should feel free and relaxed and let the conditioning of the mind arise. With awareness and attention, the practitioner can observe the different emotions that arise in the mental space. Sometimes the mental factors are going to be based on the presence of virtues in the mind. When the individual observes the presence of the virtues, the awareness in the mind makes sure that the individual does not get associated with their presence. One understands the presence of virtues in human existence as a natural process of the mind. With the presence of any virtue that arises in the mental sphere, the individual develops a sense of humility toward the existence, bringing out the seeds of virtue and flowering them that lie deep in the consciousness of human existence. Knowing that the virtues are going to create and provide the mental strength and support for the mind to tackle and understand the workings and effects of the conditioned mind. The habit patterns of the conditioned mind are so strong that the mind needs to be strengthened and prepared to overcome them. The true practice is analyzing the conditions of the mind. The conditions of the mind are jealousy, anger, delusion, attachment, impatience, and greed. When these conditions arise in the mind, the individual has to accept their existence as a result of self-action. After acceptance, with the help of concentration, the individual needs to ask themselves the cause of the condition that has led to the rise of the emotion. One needs to continually ask this question until the concentration lasts. This continuous probing of the cause of the conditions results in the formation of a clear and sequential view of the events that have led to the manifestation of the emotions of the conditioned mind. With this practice, the seeker is able to observe the consequences of each event and its repercussions without any interference. To observe the consequence and unfoldment of each event, the individual must be aware without any conditions of the good or the bad. The mental commentary should die down, and only the observance of the event should remain. With the unfoldment of each event, one should continually probe the intention of self-action. When the intention of self-action is probed, it leads to some reasoning that has led to the unfoldment of the event. Then the individual should again probe the cause or reasoning that had risen up in the previous event; again, one can observe an event or an experience that has caused the formation of that cause. Just as one peels multiple layers of an onion, the individual must peel down multiple layers of events and the causes that have resulted in the formation of emotions based on these causes and the events. The causes are just the conditions of the mind. As one peels down these layers of events and causes, one can narrow down the root cause of the blossoming of the emotions to the conditions of attachment, misunderstanding, and expectation. There can be many, but these three usually result in the formation of the emotions of anger, jealousy, hatred, greed, and delusion. The individual can observe the presence of attachment to one's own self-affirmations. Attachment means identifying oneself in totality with the self—affirmations. When the individual identifies oneself with self- affirmations it leads to the manifestation of misunderstanding. Misunderstanding that the self-affirmation is permanent to an individual's existence. The formation of the view of permanence leads to expectation. From expectations arise the emotions of the conditioned mind, which are anger, lust, hatred, jealousy, and greed. These emotions arise when the conditions of expectation are not met. The nature of existence is one of constant change or impermanence, which is always to be remembered. The clash between the true nature of existence and the nature of the conditioned mind, which is of the view of permanence and attachment, leads to delusion. When the individual starts to compare each and every event or the cause of the event with the basic or true nature of existence, the true knowledge of wisdom arises. Wisdom makes sure that the individual is free from the conditions of the mind. The wisdom of impermanence of the self—affirmations arise from experience rather than superficial rote learning. The virtue of non-attachment arises. The virtue of equanimity arises. All these virtues arise while analyzing the self with respect to the conditions of one's own being.

The human is also a social animal; the individual needs to analyze the interactions one has with the elements of society. The true nature of existence is that every individual is born to experience one's own karmic conditionings. The karmic conditionings of no two people can ever be the same. This makes the existence of each and every individual possible on various different levels of vistas. This difference in vistas leads to different knowledge and habit patterns based on the same object of existence. The difference in knowledge gained from the same object leads to differences of opinion and misunderstanding between individuals. The root cause of the misunderstanding is a lack of ability to understand the differences between individual karmic conditions. The cause of the misunderstanding is expectation, where each and every individual expects the second person to see and understand the object of knowledge not from their own vistas but from the vistas, they expect them to see. For the second person to leave their own self-affirmations, which are a result of the karmic conditionings, is usually a task of fear and anxiety as each individual is attached to one's own self-affirmation and thinks that as the true reality, so the action of leaving one's own vistas and going and observing the object from the vistas of the second person rarely happens, which results in sustenance of the misunderstanding and incompetency between individuals. It is also important to address the fact that the difference in vistas is due to the difference in karmic conditionings, and for two people to have the same outlook on an object, it is never possible as the natural law of different karmic conditionings cannot be altered. When one meditates on the conditionings and then compares them with the true nature of existence, there arises knowledge of wisdom. The wisdom of the presence of different karmic conditionings belonging to individuals and the conditions of the mind to expect that all the individuals can have the same knowledge base based on a particular object can never be met completely.

This wisdom gives rise to the virtue of non-attachment. This wisdom gives rise to the virtue of love. This wisdom gives rise to the virtue of humility. The wisdom of reality helps the individual settle down and accept the truth of life in an easy manner rather than dueling with it. With the practice of meditations, it is possible to develop wisdom by contemplating and analyzing the conditions of the mind with respect to the natural law of life, making the walk on the path of the monk-mind meaningful where the virtues of human existence become a natural state of existence. The truth of life is the unfoldment of karmic conditions. With the practice of meditation, one is able to remove the barrier of the conditioned mind from obstructing the flow of the karmic conditionings. There is total acceptance and awareness without any set conditions in the mind. This makes the mind more flexible and malleable, and one becomes simple and, in a true sense, transforms into a monk.

Practices regarding discipline, relaxation, concentration, and meditation have been discussed. Each practice has a significant role in transforming the way of life of the individual. There is only total understanding involved with awareness in all the practices. The practices are aimed at transformation or evolution rather than imposing new creations into the existence of the mind, body, and breath. The transformation happens with the purification of the habit patterns of the body, mind, and breath. Purification is to evolve from the habit patterns of the conditioned mind and slowly yet steadily adapt to the way of the natural mind state, or the monk-mind state. Through the practice of discipline, the individual is putting effort into evolving into the gross form of existence, which is the body. Even though the practices involve working with the mind and the breath, tangible change occurs in the habit patterns of the body, which eventually do percolate into the mind and breath spheres of existence. The practice of concentration brings about a tangible change in the habit patterns of the breath. The breath pattern of the conditioned mind is evolved into a natural breathing pattern where the breath controls the functioning of the body and the mind in such a way that conditions of concentration are created. Finally, with the practice of meditation, one trains the subtlest form of existence, which is the mind. The mind is where the conditions of existence lie. The working of the mind is evolved from thinking and associating to the habit patterns of the conditioned mind by just being aware and observing the workings of the conditions and then comparing them with the natural law of life. This gives rise to wisdom, where the virtues that are dormant become active in the sphere of existence. The virtuous mind is the natural state of mind, or the monk-mind. The effort to transform the habit patterns of the body, mind, and breath happens simultaneously. The three-fold effort to work on these factors of existence makes the process of transformation easy and effective, as the old habit patterns of the body, breath, and mind are so strong that transformation must take place at each level of existence to evolve from them.

After the understanding of the practices, one needs to understand the basic insights that make the experiences of the practices and the way of life more impactful and coherent to the development of the monk-mind state.

Awareness

The understanding of the insight of awareness helps in maintaining the balance between practices and the functions of day-to-day life. The nature of the monk – mind is to eliminate the difference between the functions of day-to- day life and spiritual practices. The isolation between the two is removed with an understanding of the virtue of awareness. Awareness ensures that the functions of everyday life support the practices, while the wisdom understood during the practices gets translated into daily actions. On the basis of awareness, practices flourish. That is why the understanding of the insight of awareness is of utmost importance.

Awareness is the insight of pure observance. With observance, it means that there is zero judgment. The conditions of good, bad, personal, and impersonal are kept aside. There is only viewing of the objects. The object can be a mental object, the breath, the body, or just the observance of day-to- day actions. Just as a gatekeeper observes without any conditions the incoming and outgoing vehicles, awareness also acts as a gatekeeper for the arising and passing away phenomena of the nature of existence. With awareness, one can observe the arising and passing away of sensations in the body parts, the cycle of inhalation and exhalation, and the arising and passing away of mental factors. Awareness is a tool by which the mentality of the mind gets shifted to observe the natural state of existence. With practice, the individual can also see the unfoldment of one's own karmic conditionings in the present.

The monk's mental state is the mentality of the present. The mind, due to the habit patterns of the conditions, roams around in the space of the past and the future. The insight of awareness brings the mind into the present. The act of observance only happens in the present. The habit of making judgments about any object is based on the mental factors that reside in the past or that have certain expectations for the future. But the insight of awareness is to bring the mind into the existence of the present. In the present, there is no presence of any judgment but only the pure act of observance. The pure observance of the present state of existence is awareness. With the development of the insight of awareness into practice, it leads to the mind becoming alert and sensitive to all the changes that happen in the present. The alertness leads to a sensitive state of mind, where the mind becomes sensitive to all the changes that occur in the object of awareness. With the development of sensitivity to the changes in the object, the mind becomes attentive. The attentive mind manifests itself in a state of concentration. But for the mind to become aware, it has to be trained during all times of existence rather than only during the time of the practices. Awareness could be maintained by many factors. Awareness through remembrance, attention, observation, and absorption can be practiced in everyday actions or duties.

Awareness as remembrance

Individuals more often than not become engrossed in participating in the duties that come along with their self-affirmations. The affinity for the duties of the self-affirmations makes one identify with the self-affirmations as a whole of one's existence. The practice of awareness as remembrance makes the individual mind accustomed to the law of existence through remembrance. Individuals living in the world have to participate and accomplish the duties of self-affirmations; the time to participate in practices is very limited. After practicing in the given time of isolation of the practices, the individual finds implementing the mind to the duties of the self-affirmations difficult. This happens due to a lack of awareness while fulfilling the duties of the self—affirmations. This brings about a difference in the way of one's existence, which is usually spiritual and worldly. The insight of awareness is to unite the two worlds. One should be able to see the practice in isolation as a way of nurturing the mind while fulfilling the duties in the sphere of one's self—affirmations, while the objects that rise up while participating in the self—affirmations are an exercise to increase the depth of awareness during the practices that one undertakes in isolation with respect to the world.

While participating in self-affirmations one should always remember that the present self-affirmation is not permanent and will not last forever. With remembrance, one will not totally identify one's existence with self-affirmation. The remembrance must be done while the situations are favorable as well as unfavorable while participating in the duties. Usually, one reflects on the impermanence only when the situations are unfavorable, but the insight of remembrance is to remember at all times about the true nature of existence. The true nature is impermanence, or constant change. When one remembers the impermanence of the self - affirmations the mind arrives into the present, and the practice of awareness takes place. With awareness of impermanence, the condition of expectation ceases. If one is not able to remember the nature of existence, one can bring the mind to observe the cycle of inhalation and exhalation of the breath. The cycle of breathing can be observed while bringing attention to the nostrils or to the inflation and deflation in the abdominal region. Then one can contemplate while observing the continuous pace of inhalation and exhalation in impermanence. The thought of impermanence can be translated to the existence of one's own self—affirmations. With habit, this contemplation can become a part of daily life. For a period of a minute or so, the individual can contemplate the nature of the self—affirmations. This contemplation can be repeated at regular intervals until the understanding of the law of nature gets written into the mental space. Remembrance supports not only the functions of daily life but also nourishes the spiritual practices undertaken in isolation.

Awareness as Absorption

The self-affirmations are the product of the unfoldment of the karmic conditionings. One has to experience the karmic conditionings by attending to the duties of self-affirmations, as there is no getting away from them. The individual has to experience all the situations that arise from self- affirmations. The experience could be favorable or unfavorable. Yet the individual has to experience them all. There is no escape from the karmic unfolding. If one tries to shy away from the entitled experiences, they get piled up and will have to be experienced in some form or another in the future. To be in synchronization with the will of nature or to achieve monk-mind status, the individual has to finish experiencing the karmic conditionings that have been stored due to one's own actions. The storage of the karmic conditionings takes place when one acts under the influence of the conditioned mind. The insight of absorption as awareness is to experience the karmic unfoldment in totality without the presence of the conditioned mind. The aim of the insight of absorption is to experience the karmic conditions without creating any further balance of actions.

Usually, due to the presence of the conditioned mind, the individual does not accept one's own karmic conditions and, as a result, does not immerse in the duties of the self and the affirmations that arise from them. When the experience of the individual's karmic conditions is left residual, it again becomes a reason for the manifestation of self-affirmation related to it. With awareness of the unfoldment of the karmic conditionings, the individual immerses into the duties of the self—affirmations. Each and every action regarding self-affirmation is done with total immersion into its duties. The constant awareness of actions while participating in the duties of self- affirmation is insight into awareness through absorption. The individual, without judging the experiences based on the actions or repercussions of the self-affirmations, gets immersed in accomplishing the duty expected. The individual does not shy away from the unfavorable experiences related to self- affirmation but accepts them as an opportunity to experience the karmic unfoldment and be emancipated from the existence of the condition, which may arise in one form or another in the future or in the present. The insight of awareness as absorption in the self-affirmations ensures the individual rises over the existence of the self-affirmations and unites with the will of existence as a whole.

Awareness as Observation

Awareness of interactions in daily life is an important factor in translating awareness into practices. As both the interactions and practices are interconnected, one cannot isolate the habit patterns of day-to-day interactions from the practice undertaken in isolation. Awareness during everyday interactions is developed by understanding awareness through observation. The practice of mere observation without the mental commentary of the conditioned mind is meant by awareness as observation. Usually, the mental commentary of the conditioned mind is meant by the emotion of expectation and attachment to the objects of the world. The mental chatter is due to the mind wavering in the past and the future while also being subjected to the expectations of culture, society, and race. A moviegoer watches a movie with an expectation of the flow of the story the moviegoer expects it to be. On the basis of the expectation, the moviegoer classifies the movie as good or bad and classifies the experience according to the interaction of the expectation of the movie with the actual plot of the movie shown. At the same time, an individual with no idea or background in story-telling and who is least interested in the story of his own but is interested in the story the director wants to show will have a totally different view of the same movie. As the second individual will not employ the conditions of the mind to come in between the experience of the movie being watched, the individual, one who is free of the interruption of the conditioned mind, only observes the movements of the characters with respect to the actual plot that is being unfolded by the view of the storyteller. One does not associate one's own expectation of the movie plot unfolding by just observing each and every frame or instance of the movie independently. Independent observation is to associate each and every event or frame of the movie with the previous event that has actually been undertaken in the flow of the movie rather than comparing it to the movie that has unfolded in the conditioned mind of the individual. The act of true observance takes place when one enjoys the movies without bringing in the conditions of the mind, and that happens when the individual is only observing the story the characters are portraying.

Everyday interactions take place in the mental sphere and then get translated into the physical sphere of existence. During the isolated practice of meditation and concentration, the activities in the physical sphere are absent, where the mental objects can get translated. The main practice during isolated meditation practices is to be aware of the mental factors that unfold because the mind does not need to engage in being aware of the physical interactions due to the absence of interactions in it. In isolated mediation practices, one can train the mind to be aware of the mental factors that arise and to understand them properly, so when they arise in everyday interactions, the mind is ready to use them appropriately on the basis of virtues rather than the factors of the conditioned mind. In everyday interactions, it is often difficult to be aware of the mental factors due to the multitude of objects and conditions in the mental and physical spheres that need to be addressed.

To develop awareness, observance is to observe day-to- day actions in their present moment. One needs to bring the mind from wavering into past experiences and expectations of the future into the present state of existence. If the individual in the present state is cleaning utensils, the individual should remove the mind from wavering into the past and the future and bring it into the present and observe each and every movement regarding the cleaning of utensils. There should only be the act of cleaning that the mind is observing. When there is only the act of observance of cleaning, it makes the mind quiet from the chatter of the conditioned mind. This peace and quiet mind are the quiet of the Himalayas and caves where true monks practice awareness that has to be manifested in every individual's life. The quiet achieved in day-to-day interactions also translates into the practices undertaken in isolation. The quiet ensures that a wholesome mental state is maintained at all times, rather than only during isolated practices. The mental state during interactions in the world and while practicing in isolation is complementary to each other. It is not possible to have deeper understanding and awareness during isolated practices while being unaware and careless during interactions in the world. The practice of awareness as observance is important to go deep into the mental faculties as it ensures that the mind is in the present state of existence. The individual, being aware of the physical interactions in everyday life through mere observance of them, induces a calm and quiet mind. This calm and quiet mind then propagates the individual to be aware of the mental factors during the practice in isolation. The complementary behavior of awareness as observation in the mental and physical spheres of existence needs to be understood and experienced through practice. This awareness takes time to understand and translate into daily habit patterns, as the effect of the conditioned mind is strong and needs to be worked upon continually through perseverance and the presence of the right intention to develop and manifest the monk-mind in oneself.

The insight of awareness is very important to understand, as it offers a stable ground for the practices and also helps in manifesting the virtues in the individual. The duality the individual creates of labeling objects as spiritual and the worldly ceases to exist. When awareness takes over the mind, each and every action is seen as an effort to excavate the virtues that lie blanketed under the envelope of the conditioned mind. When the duality is erased, the existence of the individual becomes simple and natural, as there is no made-up depiction of one's existence. There is unity and transparency that arise in all forms of existence. To maintain awareness at all times, the individual needs to have a strong and clear intention to affirm the practices and insights. The insight of intention is discussed in the next chapter.

Intention

The path of the monk – mind many times is a difficult one to walk. This happening is due to the absence of distancing from the habit patterns of the conditioned mind. The habits are so strong that a distance from them makes the individual very uncomfortable. The uneasiness caused by the discomfort usually makes the individual fall back into the habit patterns of the conditioned mind, as it is easy to confirm to them. For one to walk on the path of the monk – mind the intention that has led the individual to do so has to be clear and understood deeply. When the habit patterns of the conditioned mind attack the existence of the individual, the individual can reflect on the intention with which the journey on the path of the monk-mind started. With constant reflection on the intention, it provides strength to persevere through the habit patterns of the conditioned mind. With perseverance, one can endure on the path of the monk's mind according to the maximum capacity of the individual's mental and physical being. The individual who lives in society also has to endure the expectations and habit patterns of the society that govern at a given point in time.

Not all the expectations or habit patterns of society are conducive to developing the monk-mind at an individual point of existence. Society is a collection of the habit patterns of the individuals who exist under the influence of the conditioned mind. The rules and regulations that govern the existence of society therefore may not always be conducive for the individual to walk on the path of the monk-mind. The individual has to build up a habit based on reflection on the intention with which one has started the journey on the path of the monk-mind. Reflection on the intention to achieve the natural state of mind and on the rules and regulations of society, and this reflection, when compared, can lead the individual to see through the vanity and only accept those conditions that are conducive to walking on the path of the conditioned mind. Conditions that are not conducive to individual growth must not be looked down upon by the individual, as they become a cause for arrogance. The mere acceptance of the presence of those conditions and distancing from them is enough for one to be free from their effects. The reflection on the intention acts as a constant reminder for the individual to walk on the path without straying from it by coming under the influence of the conditioned mind.

Reflection on Intention

When a conflict arises between the habit patterns of the conditioned mind and the monk-mind, reflection on intention helps the individual to check the overweighing of the conditioned mind on oneself. The basic intention of the individual to walk the path of the monk – mind is to be simple. The constant reflection on being simple in all levels of existence is important for it to translate into enduring on the path of the monk-mind for a considerable amount of time. The condition of expectation and the view of permanence in the self-affirmations that lead to the manifestation of emotions like greed, anger, jealousy, hatred, and delusion, one needs to remind oneself that these conditions are far from being simple. These conditions are not to be satisfied by the monk's mind. The real existence of humanity lies in being simple and understanding that the conditions of the mind can never be satisfied. If only one needed to satisfy the conditions, there was no need to follow the path of the monk-mind. The monk's mind is based on the eradication of the effects of the conditioned mind. Whenever situations in day-to-day interactions arise where the conditions of society overweigh the true essence of the individual's existence, it is necessary for the individual to reflect on the intention of each and every action. The sanctioned reactions and responses to a situation set up by society are not always weighed in by the true intentions of the monk-mind or the natural state of mind. One needs to always check in on every reaction and response to see if it has been affected by any conditions of society or the conditions developed by the true nature of oneself alone. The individual must reflect on being free from all conditions of expectations and permanence while reacting and responding to any situation, be it mental or physical. If the individual finds any obstruction of conditions in reacting and responding, then awareness arises of the presence of a conditioned mind. At that given time, the individual can practice the virtue of patience and remain silent. When, in due course, the conditions have subsided, clarity arises about the true nature of the situation. With the clarity of the nature of situations comes a clear and needed response or reaction to the situation. At times, the response and reaction to the situation may not fulfill the criteria of the sanctioned responses and reactions set up by society. The individual, being true to one's own knowledge, develops courage as an essential virtue of the monk—the mind to stick to one's understanding. The virtue of courage ensures that even though society is against individual action, if the responses and reactions are without any conditions of the mind, one needs to be true to the understanding one has and follow it through action. There is no denial that the individual is evolving in their understanding of true intention as time progresses. The individual develops the courage to accept any mistakes made in the understanding of the intention by being truthful in its practice and aware of its consequences. Then the individual can tackle the emotion of self-loathing by understanding that, the process of understanding and practicing true intention is a continuous process and that it takes time and experience to understand it deeply. This builds up courage to persevere on the path of the monk-mind, whether one has to endure conditions built up by self-neglect or set up by society.

In simple words, each and every action of the individual should be based on the contemplation of virtues in life. With the basis of virtues for actions, the individual becomes simple. The thought process of each action should be based on a reflection on the qualities of non-violence, selflessness, kindness, and empathy. When actions are based on the reflection of these qualities, then the mind is said to be simple. The mental formations formed based on these qualities make the mind simple. As mental formations result in physical action, the totality of the individual's existence becomes simple. Being simple and natural is the way of the monk-mind. The constant reflection of each and every action based on these qualities ensures that the individual is walking the path of the monk-mind. The beauty of the individual's simplicity then translates to the near and dear ones. As the simple behavior of the individual acts as a mirror of aspirations and understanding of the other, there develops a harmonious bond of trust and love. The understanding between the two becomes such that a deep faith is cultivated in each other's existence. This faith is a result of the elimination of judgment based on the conditioned mind between the two individuals. Even when there is action that has taken place with true intention, in practical life, there are still going to be misunderstandings that arise between two individuals. The power of the practice of consolidating actions with true intentions is that, in the long term, individuals are able to see through those misunderstandings. When individuals are able to move past each other, then forgiving each other becomes easy and natural. When individuals are able to forgive each other's actions by understanding their true intentions, a very wholesome space is created between them. The freedom of acceptance and faith in the space of understanding created by individuals becomes a part of the society one is a part of. The beautiful space of acceptance and freedom created by society gets translated into a safe space for the development of a nation. This nation is an integral part of the world as a whole. The peace and freedom of acceptance and faith developed by the nation as a whole get translated into the world. With this vast expanse of interconnected individuals, the reflection of right intention leads to the formation of superior mental states. The understanding of true intentions deepens with the practice of daily reflections. The practice of daily reflections is discussed in the next chapter.

Daily Reflections

To evolve a true understanding of intentions and translate them into daily life, the individual needs to practice the insight of daily reflections. The habit of reflecting on the actions the individual has undertaken during the course of the day helps in purifying the understanding of true intention. With the evolving understanding of intentions through awareness, one brings them into action. The habit of reflecting on actions with a newly developed understanding of intention makes the individual go deeper into understanding the true intention and its working. True intention is based on the development of virtues that lead to the formation of mental factors such as non-violence, selflessness, kindness, truthfulness, honesty, and empathy. The individual needs to balance each and every action on the scale based on these mental factors. With these daily reflections, the individual can root all their actions in these factors and go deeper into their understandings and ramifications.

The practice of daily reflections

The practice of daily reflections can be done before the day begins and also when the day ends.

When the day begins, the individual can enter into active interactions with the affirmations of being aware of the mental factors of non-violence, selflessness, kindness, truthfulness, honesty, and empathy and base each and every interaction and action on them. One always needs to remind oneself about the existence of these qualities and act accordingly. The situations in life at all times are not going to favor the individual, but it is during these unfavorable situations that one has to remind oneself to act according to these qualities. The individual must also forgive themselves for all the actions and interactions that did not adhere to these qualities. True forgiveness is being aware of the happenings that have taken place without being aware of these qualities and making sure that they do not repeat again. If some happenings do repeat, then the individual must make sure that the intensity is at least reduced. With this remembrance and reflection, one can enter into the duties of the self—affirmations.

The practice of daily reflections can be undertaken when the day ends. This is the time just before going to sleep. Before falling asleep, the individual needs to go through the happenings of the day. With awareness developed, one can remember the happenings of the day. The interactions, reactions, and responses one had to all types of situations, which were favorable, unfavorable, and had no particular significance, must be remembered. The individual must weigh all the interactions and actions against the qualities of non-violence, selflessness, kindness, truthfulness, honesty, and empathy. The individual should question themselves about whether all their reactions and responses are based on these qualities or not. Whether the mind was able to accept all the happenings in their true nature of existence? Whether all the reactions and responses to situations were based on the conditions of expectations and permanence? When one reflects in this way on the understanding of intentions and their actions in daily life, the quality of responses and reactions improves with each day of one's existence in this world. Not all actions and reactions are going to be perfect for any individual. But the perseverance of observing the imperfections in one and analyzing them helps improve the way the mind works in a natural way. After reflecting on the actions and interactions of that particular day, the individual should affirm that the next day is going to be a new morning, not only in the physical sense but also in the sense of a better understanding of the true intentions of human existence. All the analyzed actions and interactions that need to be perfected will have priority to undergo maximum awareness in action. The priority is to be aware that the actions that are not in line with the true intentions fall in line with the intentions. As the existence of human mentality is not perfect, actions may slip into the old habit patterns of the conditioned mind. But the constant reflection of each and every action and introspection on the true intentions on a daily basis protects the mind from slipping on the path of the conditioned mind. The constant habit of daily reflections helps in providing enthusiasm to walk the path of the monk-mind. The enthusiasm arises from the knowledge that has been gained from the habit of constant reflection, where the individual can see the change in their own actions and interactions with themselves and society at large. The enthusiasm then creates inroads for the development of faith on the path of the monk's mind, as the individual can perceive visible results in one's own behavior.

This concludes the section on the practice and the insight part of the path of development of the monk's mind. It is important to remember that the main intent of this section is to develop a mind that is enriched by virtues. The virtues are excavated by the practices and insights that lie deep in the caves of human existence. That is why the practices and insights aim to dispel the notion of duality, which is both spiritual and worldly. It is the unification of these two existences that enriches human existence. The cessation of duality between the spiritual and the non-spiritual is developed by amalgamating or merging practices with insight. Without insight, practices become only a physical exercise, and insight without practice becomes hollow or empty knowledge as it is not enriched by experience. The practices and insights go hand in hand and are complimentary to each other. The unification of these two ensures that each and every single moment of existence is an opportunity to develop the monk-mind with the right intention. With the development of the monk-mind, the true intention of existence starts working through the individual, thus making sure that the individual has become one with the totality of existence and has evolved into higher states of being.

To go deeper into understanding the practices and insights, one should develop a monk lifestyle. To develop a monk lifestyle, it is not necessary to leave the duties in the world and go deep into forests or the Himalayas, but to undertake in essence the lifestyle of the monk. These are the factors of the monk lifestyle that one needs to bring into daily practice.

Factors of a Monk Lifestyle

The monk-mind is developed with the extraction of virtues; the virtues are developed with the practices and insights, and the practices and insights are developed with the inculcation of the factors of the monk lifestyle into daily habits and behavioral patterns. The monk practices certain lifestyle patterns in daily life. These lifestyle practices can be deeply understood and translated into the everyday life of the individual claiming to walk on the path of the monk-mind. One might fear that these lifestyle practices may include the shunning of wealth, comforts, and interactions with loved ones. These are not the real factors of the monk life, as these are mere external exhibitions that do not relate to the reality of the monk life. If an individual really understands the factors of the monk life, then these factors can be translated into the daily life of any individual. The factors make the individual simple and ensure that the individual practicing them goes deep in the understanding of practices and insights.

These factors of the monk lifestyle may seem insignificant, but rest assured that they ensure that the individual really evolves from the habit patterns of the conditioned mind. The main aim of the book is to transform the individual into a monk in totality rather than focusing only on selective parts of the monk's life. To be a monk is a state of existence rather than a confirmation of any religion or a holy book. It is a basic state of existence where anybody can transform one's state of existence without coming under any influence of culture, region, religion, or a book. Just as the mango fruit grown in India is called an Indian mango and the mango grown in Brazil is known as a Brazilian mango, in the same way one must develop into a monk initially, then confirm to any religion, region, or holy book. Just as seen in the case of the Brazilian and Indian mangoes, it is important to have the mango in the first place to be classified into different types. The factors of monk life ensure that the individual, irrespective of any region, religion, or culture, transforms into a monk. A monk who is necessarily a fiber of society and respects its identity and presence in individual life. These are the universal factors that help transform the individual into a monk. The practice of these factors sets the individual apart from the normal and conditioned functioning of society.

Factors of a monk lifestyle

1. Silence

2. Solitude

3. Association

4. Self – sufficiency

5. Service

6. Prayer

7. Friendship

Silence

The picture the mind paints of a monk is usually sitting in forests and Himalayan peaks with eyes closed and a calm reflection of peace and serenity reflecting on the monk's face. It is the silence of the forests and the vast expanse of the mountain peaks and cave enclosures that have translated into the being of the monk. It is important to remember that there is no complete silence in the space of the forests and the mountain peaks, as there is sound made by birds and insects, the movement of tree leaves due to wind, the flow of river water or a brook, etc., yet how do these places provide a conducive environment for attaining silence? It is important to understand that the silence here refers to the silence of any artificial or conditioned interactions in that space. There is only the natural movement of existence. There is a feeling of stillness that supports this natural movement, which provides a conducive space for the monk to be silent. This stillness of the natural movement translates into the being of the monk. The stillness is the reason for the silence that the monk exhibits in his being. It is the nourishment that the monk has received from the stillness of the natural movement that induces silence in all aspects of the monk's being. The stillness in the space gets converted into the stillness of the monk's being. Stillness does not mean total inactivity, but the natural movement of the body, mind, and breath. When the body, mind, and breath move in their natural movements, it leads to silence. For the monk to incorporate this natural movement, it is required for the monk to train himself in the space of natural movement. The space is created by the natural surroundings of the forests and the mountain peaks. Usually, after completing a retreat in the natural surroundings, the monk returns to the world. After the return, the monk usually notices that, as time passes, the stillness and silence start to lessen, and again, the noise of the artificial or conditioned surroundings starts effecting the existence of the monk. The difference between the monk and any lay individual who is participating in the daily duties of the world vanishes. If there is any difference, it is only the outer appearance that distinguishes the monk from any lay individual. To continue to live in the forests and mountain peaks is not possible at all times to maintain that silence of stillness. At some point in time, the monk or any individual who is participating in a retreat in these natural surroundings has to enter the world to participate in the duties assigned by its existence.

But it is the duty of the monk or the individual to replicate that stillness of silence of the retreat even while undertaking the duties in the world. The absence of proper understanding of the stillness in the natural environment is the cause of its termination when the individual or the monk return to society. The improper understanding arises when the individual escapes into the forests or mountain retreats for silence. The stillness of silence has to be developed inside the human consciousness rather than only depending on external factors. The space of stillness provided by nature has to be replicated inside one's mental being rather than only depending on the external environment. When the individual returns to the duties of the world, the silence can be sustained for longer periods of time.

Everyone cannot afford to seclude themselves in forests or the mountain peaks for a silent retreat. Yet there has to be some way to develop the silence without actually escaping the duties of the world. The basis of silence is mental silence, which has been discussed in the section on practices and insights. The silence in the physical world needs to be understood and practiced so that it enriches the silence in the mental realm. The silence in the physical and vocal realms has to be understood in order to nourish the mental silence. At the same time, verbal and physical silence is not a forced silence but an understanding of when to be active in these spheres of existence and when to be inactive. That is why the common misconception of silence as inactivity and reservedness in these realms needs to be addressed. When one forces inactivity as a misconception in the verbal and physical realms of existence, it becomes a cause for suppression of all the conditions that have arisen in the mental sphere. The suppressed conditions due to the forced clamping of the physical and verbal realms make a way for creating a delusion of one's own existence, which in turn gives rise to fear and anxiety. The presence of an inability to handle anxiety and fear due to improper manifestations of silence may produce physical as well as severe mental ailments. The aim of silence is to be naturally still, to observe the rising of the conditions of the mind, and to act on them in a natural way. The natural way is based on the natural law of existence, which is the constant change or impermanence of the state of existence of the objects in the world. According to this law of existence, there is a proper and natural response that the situations and objects in the world are awaiting from the individual. The exact and concurrent response to situations can be known by the individual through the true practice of silence. In reality, the natural actions and responses to each and every situation and object of the world are, in a true sense, the practice of silence. For this action to take place in existence, the individual needs to develop a sense of when to act and when not to act. This cycle of activity and inactivity needs to be brought into the habit patterns of the individual.

The practice of Silence

The practice of silence relates to the physical and verbal realms of the individual. In the early stages of practice, the individual must take some time from the daily routine to be quiet verbally. The practice of silence during that period of time should not affect the duties one has to carry out. It should not cause discomfort to people in association with the individual. If one is not habituated to being quiet, then this practice in the initial stages is going to be difficult. Slowly and steadily, the period of silence can be increased. One should keep aside some part of the day where one is calm and quiet without interfering in any outward action. The silence can be maintained while performing one's own duties, where there is no requirement for any verbal interaction. With practice, the individual can experience longer durations of peace and tranquility. With the absence of any verbal interaction during this time period, there is no loss of energy. The abundance of energy in the individual can prove to be a reason for the experience of calmness and tranquility. An individual cannot maintain high standards of awareness and concentration with constant leakage in the energy flow. The basis of the monk's mind is to maintain awareness at all times, and for maintaining this awareness, the practice of silence plays an important part. Silence plugs the leak of energy.

One of the root causes of misunderstandings and rifts between individuals is habitual verbal interactions. What are the habitual verbal interactions? It is the habit of voicing one's opinion and expectations when not asked for. The habit of voicing one's opinion and expectations is the habit of the conditioned mind. Individuals who do not practice silence also have the habit of giving advice when not called for. Individuals who are not content with themselves or do not have an aim for developing their own mental existence tend to employ their time, energy, and space to create the opinions of other individuals. This leads to the habit of gossiping. The habit of gossiping when exercised portrays that the individual is not interested in self-development but has the time and audacity to judge the other person.

The individual needs to distance himself from this frivolous behavior of the mind. With the practice of silence in daily life, one is able to cut down on unwanted interactions. These unwanted verbal interactions are a habit of the conditioned mind where the individual is seeking outside support for self-gratification. By maintaining verbal silence, the individual can observe one's own karmic unfoldment and the reactions of society to it. This gives rise to wisdom in the individual to know and be aware of the moments in situations where one should speak up or remain silent. By maintaining silence, the individual becomes aware of the natural law of existence. With awareness of the natural law of existence, which is of constant change and impermanence, the individual suits himself or herself to the best situations to be verbal and vocal about. The selective nature of the mind for choosing situations is the result of the practice of silence. Silence not only helps in choosing situations to be vocal or verbal about but also in choosing what to be verbal about. With awareness of the natural law of existence, the individual is able to see the progression of events through the practice of silence. In the progression of events, one is able to see which events and what the event really needs to affect the situations in a manner to develop one's mental state into the monk-mind state. This is the power of silence, where the individual is able to use the power of inactivity to turn each and every moment into a higher mental state.

The practice of silence helps in developing the virtue of patience. With the practice of silence, the individual can observe the happenings and respond to the happenings based on the natural law of existence. The practice of response is the true nature of the virtue of patience, as discussed before. Rather than reacting to a situation, with the development of understanding silence, the individual starts to respond to any situations or happenings. With the presence of proper responses to situations and the objects of the world, the individual, even though meddling in the duties of the self, affirmations is successful in shunning the unwanted noise of reactions, which is the habit pattern of the conditioned mind.

The fact that the silence of the forests and mountains cannot be retained in the usual hectic world is an accepted fact. It is of course necessary to duplicate the stillness of these natural surroundings into the levels of human existence. That is why the individual should make sure that there is time taken out to be in natural surroundings for a period of time without any disturbance. At least once a year, a period of silent retreat in the mountains or monasteries should be kept aside. But it is important to understand that the stillness of these natural surroundings cannot last long if the individual or even the monk sees them as an escape route from the uneasiness of the mental chatter caused by the habit patterns of the conditioned mind. The true practice of silence during day-to-day interactions has to be maintained so that the emotion of escapism does not rise up. With the practice of silence, there is a basic presence of stillness that appears in the mental space, even though it may not be as deep as one experiences in their natural surroundings. The presence of stillness should be such that it does not lead to escapism from the day-to-day routine of life.

The silence of physical actions is not discussed, as it will be understood in the next chapter of solitude. The everyday practices of relaxation, concentration, and meditation help maintain stillness and awareness of all physical actions. Just as the monk who roams in silence or establishes one's existence in the beauty of silence, the individual who aspires to walk the path of the monk's mind should dissolve into the beauty of silence as it provides strength, which develops into immunity from the conditions of the mind.

Solitude

As discussed in the earlier chapter on silence, a monk's existence is usually visualized in solitude rather than in places of human congestion. One aspect of solitude is to provide the right conditions for inducing stillness and silence in the monk or the individual. At the same time, solitude provides a space for reflection and distancing from the conditions of society and the expectations that the individual has built for themselves. The true importance of solitude needs to be understood in order to maximize its utility; otherwise, it could be seen as an escape route from the duties of the everyday world.

The individual who is immersed in the duties of the self—affirmations—gets too involved in them, forgetting the aim and purpose of one's own existence. The purpose is to attain a natural state of mind. In isolation, the individual is able to reflect on and observe one's own actions and see the effect of the conditions on themselves. The question arises: can an individual who is immersed in the duties of the world really afford to isolate themselves? The practice of the monk who isolates oneself has to be understood in its true essence to really practice isolation; otherwise, it would be mere escapism from the inability to perform the duties of the world. The truth of existence is that everyone is born alone and has to leave the world alone. One is born in this world due to the causes or karmic conditions created by one's own actions. At the same time, one leaves this world with the impressions of one's actions left in the mind during the time period of existence. The impressions of these actions and the present state of existence are the factors that guide one's state of living. The state of living or existence is of pure independence. As discussed earlier, the individual who is immersed in one's own conditions and the conditions of society becomes so engrossed or lost in the duties and conditions that he or she becomes unaware of the self's true state of being. The intimacy of the conditions of the self and society makes it believable to the individual that the true nature of existence is only in satisfying these conditions and duties. This creates a false sense of dependency on the conditions of oneself as well as of society. The sense of dependency then becomes a cause of sorrow and grief, as these conditions are not freeing but shackle the individual to the ground. There is no room for freedom, which makes the individual feel entrapped. Isolation provides a space for the individual to get a perspective on life as a whole. When the individual creates distance from the space of conditions, there arises a view on how to handle or execute them while maintaining the virtues in the mental space. The distancing of oneself from these conditionings helps the individual view all the parameters of the conditionings set up by the individual and society without any attachment. This view gives rise to the feeling of independence.

Solitude can be practiced in two ways: one while undertaking the duties in the world, and the other by removing oneself from the space where the duties take place.

The first condition is when the individual is undertaking solitude while existing within the boundaries of the self—affirmations. The practice of solitude is important to enter a space of comfort where the conditions of society are not present to produce any kind of judgment. The regular practice of relaxation, concentration, and meditation needs a dedicated space where there is no obstruction from the usual movement of the self-affirmations and the conditions of society. This dedicated space is very important for the individual to maintain to bring peace and stillness into everyday life. The only action that takes place in this dedicated space is to free the mind from the conditions and become simple. This space should act as a temple of existence where there is no obstruction to reflection and peace. It is a sanctuary for the individual to go deep into one's own mental and physical realms without getting disturbed by the hustle and bustle of everyday chaos. Just as a doctor, while performing surgery in an operation theater, is given a secluded space to perform the surgery without any disturbance from hospital activities, an individual too needs a space for seclusion. When the individual enters that space, it should signal to the other cohabiting person that it is time for the individual to be left alone. The individual entering that space needs space to perform the surgery in their own mental and physical realms, just like a doctor. This space should be the center of the individual's existence, as it creates an environment of safety and freedom for the individual. So, it is the individual who has to take up the responsibility to maintain the sanctity of the space. This space should not become a part of the space where the actions of daily routine take place, as it contaminates the space. This space has to be different from the other spaces of existence where the interactions related to daily routine or the interactions related to society take place. If this space becomes part of the space of the daily routines, it gets contaminated. This contamination is not physical; it is a subtle contamination of space where the distinction of being alone and quiet is not maintained. The space of relaxation, concentration, and meditation should only be meant to perform these activities, and it should not mix with other spaces of existence. The individual must make sure that in this space no other activities take place other than the said activities. When the individual enters this space, the body and the mind should automatically come to know that the individual has entered a space of decompression. This isolation in everyday action helps inducing the quality of peace and tranquility in everyday life.

The practice of isolation in daily life can become so integrated into habit patterns that it has the tendency to become a ritual without any awareness. The lack of awareness does not support its integration. There arises a need to move away from the habituated space to reflect and get a perspective on one's own way of life. For an individual to have an overall view of one's own habit patterns and the conditions that precede them, they have to move away from the space of their daily routine. The individual must find a suitable space where the practices of relaxation, concentration, and meditation can take place without any judgment. At the same time, the space must also provide an opportunity for the individual to reflect on one's habit patterns and adjust in such a way that the conditions of society as well as of oneself do not hamper the journey on the path of the monk – mind. One should remember that the space where one leaves should not turn into a space for escapism. It should be a voluntary decision of awareness to move away from the daily routine. To not make it an escape route is a factor one has to take into consideration. The duties of the self—affirmations—must be managed in such a way that all the responsibilities are met beforehand and the absence of the individual does not cause any discomfort to the people related to the space of that individual. While leaving for the retreat, one has to have the consent of the people with whom they deal on a day-to-day basis. It should not be an abrupt leave of absence but a conscious choice for a certain period of time to recuperate. The retreat for reflection should not be mistaken for a holiday or vacation. A holiday or vacation does not deal with mental space with the right intention. It only provides a space for enjoyment and recreation. A retreat is no space for enjoyment or recreation. It is meant to delve into a space and time for understanding one's way of life and reflecting on it to be a better and simpler individual. It has no relation to society, as usually vacations and holidays do. The truth of existence is that the individual is alone in this universe. Being alone in society is not welcomed by the standards of society. But the truth of life is that one has to accept being alone. Being alone and being lonely are two different aspects of life. The true aspect of being alone is that it makes the individual free and simple in the way he or she lives life. There is no fear, as one has accepted and is content with being the way existence has wanted one to be. But to be lonely is to compare oneself with the conditions of society, which are not true at all times. The individual feeling lonely has not accepted being in a natural state of existence and has created a habit of constant comparison. The individual with the feeling of loneliness has attributed the responsibility of being happy and peaceful to society rather than to one's own natural way of being. With the proximity of the individual to the conditions of society and the space created by it, one is not able to accept the reality of being alone. The non-acceptance of the reality of being alone causes the rise of anxiety and fear in the human mental realm. The space created by being isolated slowly and steadily helps in adjusting to the fact of being alone. The fact that relations in society are temporary and one's own actions and the understanding behind those actions are going to guide the individual in the present as well as the future. The retreat is a space where the individual accepts being alone by observing the habit patterns and conditions of the mind. With these reflections, the individual, after emerging from the retreat, must be changed in some way or another. The way one accepts one's own mental conditions, the way one responds to the situations built up by society, and so on and so forth. After the period of isolation concludes, the individual must return with a higher understanding of the practice of love, equanimity, non-attachment, and responsibility. The change or evolution must translate into the practice of awareness, concentration, and meditation. One should be able to let go of the unnecessary conditions of the mind, accept one's existence in the simplest manner, and be more in tune with the natural movements of nature.

Just as a monk who wanders in forests and Himalayan peaks in solitude, the individual should be able to understand the motive of the monk's solitude and be able to translate it into one's own life. That is the aim of understanding solitude. Just attending a retreat in solitude without any understanding should not be followed by the individual. There has to be a proper understanding of entering into a retreat. A proper understanding can be attained when the individual determines for the period of solitude that there will be a greater understanding of virtues and simplicity in the behavioral patterns of oneself. A proper aim should be set by the individual rather than a wayward approach while entering the space provided by solitude. One is able to reduce the factors of anger, jealousy, delusion, and greed.

The individual, being aware and rooted in the presence of virtues in being, becomes fearless and confident of one's own existence. This confidence is not a product of arrogance, but confidence that all the conditions thrown by existence are of one's own doing, and the answers to all those questions lie deep inside oneself. The answers are based on virtues, truly being simple, or being a monk in essence.

Association

Monkhood is usually seen as a community living. There have been numerous traditions where monks usually cohabitate in a common place. The traditions of monastic living have been passed down for ages. There might have been some thought behind this type of co-existence. Monks of the same tradition share a common way of life, a common belief system, practice, and philosophy. When monks who have a common aim for life come together, a safe space is created for the monks to grow in their understanding of practice, insight, and virtues. A harmonious co-existence is created where there is understanding of each other's karmic conditionings. The aim of living together is to be a strong support system for one another, where there is constant encouragement to walk the desired path of the respective tradition. The co-existence helps in protecting the members of the community from any misunderstandings and delusions about the path chosen. A monk who lives alone and has just started the practice and understanding of the way of monk life can easily be discouraged by the factors of delusion, sloth, and fear. The monk, until reaching a certain point of maturity on the chosen path of self-development, is susceptible to these attacks. But a strong community of like-minded monks acts as a blanket of protection until the monk reaches a level of perfection or maturity. When there is an exchange of ideas, experiences, and understandings, a space of comfort and faith is created between the monks. These exchanges often act as guiding points of encouragement and faith on the chosen path of self-development. One does not feel alone or left out on the path as difficulties arise. Some of the more experienced monks act as a shield for the novice monks by sharing their own experiences and understandings of the difficulties on the path to support them. There is also a certain camaraderie between monks across all stages of monkhood, which establishes a base of comfort in the community. The constant association of like-minded individuals keeps the space conducive to the path the monk has chosen to walk. The association determines the monk's longevity and the quality of his understanding of the chosen path.

The discipline of association among the monks should be translated into every individual's life. An individual is known by the associations he or she keeps. The company one surrounds with is a reflection of the mental state of that being. It is important to surround oneself with the right people, as the company one associates with influences the individual's way of being. Just as the company one keeps is a reflection of one's mental state, the mental state of the individuals in the company also gets absorbed by the individual. That is why it is very important to be aware and watchful of the people one surrounds with. Associations can drastically determine an individual's way of life. The associations can rapidly speed up one's progress on the path of the monk-mind as well as deter from the path as well.

The habit of right associations needs to be understood well and maintained accordingly. An individual who aspires to be a successful businessperson tends to meet and mingle with people who are interested in the profession of business. The interactions in these situations are all about the workings of business. The interactions tend to be based on the experiences and insights gained from doing business. When an aspirant who aspires to be successful in this field comes into contact with the knowledge base of individuals who are experienced and at present employ their traits in the given field, the individual's horizons widen. There is a certain clarity of thought about how to go on with business matters. There is a certain comfort level established between individuals who are in the same profession, which provides a space for the aspirant to learn and grow in the knowledge of doing the right things at the right time. In contemporary times, individuals tend to only associate with people for material enrichment or to climb the ladders of social status. But the pursuit of climbing the stairs of higher mental states goes into the background. While being immersed in material pursuits, the individual often forgets the dire need to develop higher mental states based on the existence of virtues.

Just as individuals associate with people for material and social benefits, top priority should also be given to associate with individuals who can help in developing the mind or higher mental states. It is important to understand that humans are social animals. The individual has to live in society or groups, as it is the basic or instinctive nature of human existence. That is why building awareness of associations with people is very important. Just as in a monastery, monks come together and discuss their spiritual journey, an individual must have a group or an individual where all feelings, emotions, and mental factors can be discussed openly without any judgment. To be free of any judgment is to be free from the conditions set up by society or the self. Every individual has a friend or a person to whom they can vent their personal and emotional problems, and the individual feels comfortable being in the company of that individual. The other person who is listening to the vented-out problems is just listening to the individual because of the intimacy of the relationship they both share. This is not meant by having the right associations. Not to deny the need or importance of that relationship, but in that particular scenario, the second person does not want to deal with the karmic conditions of the person who is in a dilemma in any situation or emotion. There is only the factor of making the individual in a dilemma feel better. In the scenario of the right association, that is not the case. The aim is not to make the individual feel good about anything. To have the right association is to have a space of non-judgment in totality where there is no right and wrong, good or bad. In this type of association, there has to be freedom in narrating the incident that has been the cause of a certain emotion to rise. In the narration of the incident, there is no judgment. The individuals involved in the narration and its contemplation are free to give their own interpretation of that incident without any fear of the second person liking it or not. This gives rise to the knowledge of many perspectives on a certain situation. With the rise of these perspectives, the individual involved in the situation or incident has many options for understanding or responding to the incident. And there is total freedom for the individual involved to choose any perspective the individual finds comfort in and act accordingly. There would be no judgment of any kind. In this type of association, the individuals involved create a safe space where each individual is able to understand and accept one's own true nature by being aware of individual karmic unfoldment.

Secondly, all the individuals involved in the association share a common aim of developing into higher mental states. There is always thorough contemplation on virtues and how each and every individual can grow in understanding and practicing virtues in daily life. How the presence of virtues should become a natural state of being. There is also a thorough contemplation of the defilements one has to face on the path of the monk's mind. Through honest and truthful interactions based on real emotions, one can understand the conditions of the mind. Through these honest and truthful interactions, the only aim is to overcome those through true understanding rather than suppressing them into deeper mental pockets. There is a truthful exchange of ideas and experiences for all the individuals involved in the association. The interchange of truthful and honest views and experiences without any judgment and with the common aim of being simple and developing virtues creates a healthy and wholesome space for individuals to co-exist. These associations ensure that life in general becomes easy and blissful to endure. Through these associations, one is able to experience the true meaning of love and affection. True love and affection ensure that each and every individual feels protected and safe. Safe and protected by being naturally as one is. That is why it is said that one is known by the company one keeps. If the company is judgmental and materialistic or is bound by the conditioned mind, one too starts reflecting those common traits. The influence of such a space is too heavy to withdraw from. If the space is a wholesome space where the common aim is to grow in virtues and lead a life based on the qualities of the natural mind, then the individual starts reflecting on these values and traits. This type of association makes way for a wholesome society.

It is a wholesome habit to frequent a monk who is open to any sort of discussion. Generally, monks who are not engaged in the usual self-affirmations of the world have a better perspective on life. As monks are not involved in the same way as a usual layperson, a better view and understanding could also be gained for understanding life as a whole. It is important to know the proper way to approach a monk. Usually, individuals approach monks just as an excuse to see them as a remedy to life's problems. Some sort of mysticism is involved in their presence. Just by meeting a monk or bowing down to a monk, one perceives gaining merit in the flow of life. There is a hidden expectation of gaining some merit, be it material or spiritual. This misunderstanding has to go. Not to deny giving respect to monks or their traditions. A certain respect has surely to be given to monks, as monks are the carriers of knowledge the teachers of the past or present have taught. There is a certain level of virtue in monks who have left the usual workings of the world and have traveled the path of purification, which is surely to be respected. But the understanding that simply bowing to them is enough is not sufficient. The interaction with a monk should be based on reality rather than any mythical expectations. One should interact with or see the life a monk leads and try to understand the truth behind each and every action. There should be real openness about one's mental conditionings and a true intention to understand them. One should openly voice their true aspirations in order to understand how to fulfill those aspirations or reject them. Just as a monk who is leading a simple way of life The individual must ask or contemplate the factors of simplicity with the monk on how the individual can follow the simple way of life while living in the conditioned world. Just as an individual enters the vicinity of a monk, the individual must return with a greater understanding of the virtues of life from the monk. There has to be this awareness at all times.

If an individual is not able to be in a company of people where proper reflection on the existence of virtues is possible, then it is much better to be alone. The individual can find some peace in solitude. The company of solitude can be completely relied upon, rather than being in the company of individuals who would hamper the evolution of one's own existence. One can also take refuge in nature. Being in the company of birds, animals, and trees can be a soothing experience. Being in unity with nature can also bring about drastic changes in human behavior, as there is no room for any conditions in the openness of being in nature. Association is a major factor that can make or break an individual's existence; it is one of the most important factors any individual, irrespective of culture, religion, or region, has to be aware of.

Self – Sufficiency

Self-sufficiency forms the basis of monk discipline. Monks living in isolation need to sustain themselves. The basic practices that help in the process of self-sustenance are called self-sufficiency. Assistance at all times cannot be afforded by a monk, as it may deter the seclusion and silence of the monk. To be dependent on any other individual for the basic need of sustenance is like an amputation of some kind. The monk life is meant for total freedom, but the dependency of the monk can deter the scale of freedom, and the true joy of becoming a monk can never be experienced. It is a given that no individual in the world can be independent of other individuals in society. As discussed in the previous chapter, it is an accepted fact that humans are social animals. However independent an individual may be at some point in time, they have to be dependent on each other at some point in their lives. In situations where the individual is dependent on others, there are certain situations and events in life for which the individual needs to be self-sufficient. Where the individual should not be completely dependent on the other for any sort of assistance.

Even in isolation, the monk has to take care of the body and the living quarters. If, for basic sustenance, the monk starts to be dependent on others, then the isolation will be breached. The monk has to know how to live alone, and for that, the monk has to be self-efficient. By being self-sufficient, the monk has to know how to take care of the body, food, lodgings, and clothes worn. The monk's isolation and freedom will be protected if the monk knows how to cook a meal for nutrition, how to clean clothes for hygiene, and how to clean the premises of the lodgings the monk has put up in for keeping a serene and calm mind. The novice monks that arrive in a monastery have to undergo this rigorous training where these basic practices of self-efficiency are taught first. That is why the initial stages of monk life are important, as during this time the monk starts to understand and practice the habit patterns and the skills that are required to maintain the sanctity of monk life for a long time. As the skill of being self-sufficient increases, the monk's degree of freedom in existence also increases. The skill of self-sufficiency practiced by the monks needs to be understood properly and then translated into the everyday life of every individual.

Just as the monk, individuals too are dependent on society or others to live comfortably. In some cases, though, the individual must be self-dependent or self-sufficient. In order to be able to live independently, the individual must develop these basic skill sets so that the degree of freedom in the personal and social spheres increases. The individual must learn and adapt to the skill sets that help them take care of themselves.

The individual must learn how to cook food for themselves. The food prepared should be edible and of nutritional value. It is not expected for the individual to become a professional chef, but the skill set of cooking food should be such that the taste buds approve of it to some degree and the hunger pangs in the body also diminish, while at the same time providing proper nutrition to the body. Being independent enough to know the needs of the body and prepare a nourishing meal for oneself is a very important skill to learn, as with a hungry mind, it becomes difficult to think, meditate, and reflect comfortably. Any individual should not be dependent on others to fulfill their nutrition and the feeling of hunger on the other. When one is dependent on the other, one has to succumb to the whims and wishes of the other, as at all times the other person may not fully be able to comprehend the needs of the individual. It becomes decisive for the individual to be independent in this important skill so that the agony and anger related to the dependency on this important life skill do not affect the day-to-day working of the individual.

The individual who wishes to walk the path of the monk-mind needs to be aware of basic hygiene and organizational skills. The space where one resides is seen as a temple of worship. The sanctity of the physical and subtle realms has to be maintained. The sanctity of the physical realm reflects into the subtle realm, and the sanctity of the subtle realms reflects into the physical realm. These spheres of existence are complimentary to each other. The space one lives in reflects the mental conditioning of the individual. That is why the space for living should be maintained in such a way that it provides a space for reflection and meditation. One should know how to keep the space in a way that is hygienic and organized. The hygiene and organization should reflect the mental being of the individual inhabiting them. Of course, it should not be misunderstood that only a well-organized space or a hygienic space is a true indication of a developed mind; some individuals, irrespective of state of mind, are endowed with these skills. There should be awareness involved in maintaining the space of one's existence, as it provides space and nutrition for the aspirations of one's mental space. The individual should not be dependent on the other for keeping one's own space in an orderly manner. One should manage the living space in the manner of a priest who maintains the sanctum sanctorum of a temple. The space should vibrate with the divine vibrations of virtue and calmness of the mind. One should maintain the area with the utmost hygiene and care, and for that upkeep, one should learn the required skills. The synchronization of thoughts, speech, and action must be reflected in that area. It becomes the utmost priority for the individual to keep the space with self-effort in such a way that it provides motivation to be silent and walk the path of the monk-mind.

The monk wears a particular robe or outfit that differentiates the monk's existence from the rest of the common individuals. The robe or outfit becomes part of the identity of the monk. It becomes the duty of the monk to take care of the clothes and drapes. Be it dying the robes, washing them, or stitching the worn-out or torn parts of the robe, individuals need to learn and practice the skill of maintaining the clothes or outfits they adorn. Not in its entirety as a monk maintains the robes, but in principle, the individual has to translate these skills into habit patterns of daily life. The individual must learn the skill set of washing one's own clothes and maintaining them in proper fashion. Maintaining clothes is a hygienic practice. Once again, just as the monk is responsible for the cleanliness of one's own robes and outfits, the individual must adapt to this practice and be independent and not dependent on others for the upkeep of one's own clothes. In society, it is important to have the habit of being suitably dressed, and the individual must learn how to maintain the outfit worn as it represents the character of that individual. Washing and maintaining the outfit should not become a burden for the individual but rather become a natural part of the daily habit pattern.

The above-discussed parameters are only discussed comprehensively and do not entirely cover the factors of self-sufficiency in their entirety. In short, the aim was just to give a preview of the understanding of the practice of being self-sufficient. Some of the factors are going to change according to the different times society lives in. The parameters discussed are purely rudimentary. The aim of being self-sufficient is to be independent to the highest degree possible. The practice of self-sufficiency makes one confident in one's ability to live alone. The confidence in the ability to live alone or be self-sufficient makes one enjoy freedom with a high degree of pragmatism. The basic skill set of a monk, which makes the monk independent if translated in essence rather than outer exhibitions, can even make the individual live the life of a monk while undertaking the duties of everyday life.

One might ask what cooking food, cleaning, and washing have to do with developing the monk-mind. It may seem very superficial in nature and may have no relation to really developing wholesome states of mind. All these skill sets are employed to make the individual totally independent and have the habit patterns of the monk while undertaking the duties of everyday life. It does not mean that the individual has to clean, cook, and wash at all times. That would be a gross misunderstanding. One should not know how to take care of oneself independently, as it brings in the factor of self-confidence. The self-confidence that wherever the karmic conditionings have the individual in, the individual can be independent and free. There is no need for dependency on any other individual. If, at some point in life, the individual has to delegate this practice to others, it should not be because of inability but from experience and confidence in oneself, or, in simple words, for ease of life, to focus on developing a virtuous state of being. Delegating essential habit patterns to others because of an inability to practice that skill set is a sign of weakness. Weakness arises from the conditioned mind. Until the effect of the conditioned mind is present in the individual, there can be no total mental development. With the presence of this weakness, the individual can never be sure of oneself and can never travel the path of the monk-mind with true confidence in one's being. It isn't necessary for the individual to perform these tasks themselves at all times, but the individual has to learn the skill sets and be sure enough to delegate these tasks on the basis of confidence rather than any feeling of inability.

Developing self-sufficiency also helps in aiding the growth of the virtue of courage in the individual. This is the reason monks are trained in all the facets of self-sufficiency. The monk who lives in the monastery has to take care of himself as well as take part in maintaining the upkeep of the monastery as a whole. In this process, the monk gathers a load of experience in the skill sets of being self-sufficient. There is a rise in self-confidence after developing these skill sets. The self-confidence is such that the individual becomes fearless in any situation faced.

As there is certainty of action in the individual, there is fearlessness that whatever the situation, be it favorable or unfavorable, the individual can take care of themselves appropriately without being dependent on any other individual. This helps in excavating the virtue of courage in the individual. The courage of facing all the self-affirmations in their true sense. Simultaneously, an immunity develops in the individual to understand the unfoldment of the karmic conditionings. Even though the skill sets of self-sufficiency may seem trivial in nature, they play a major role in the development of virtues and becoming a true monk in essence.

Service

Monks living in isolation or in collective monasteries depend on society for certain aspects of their lives. The society takes care of the monks' expenses, medical facilities, and so on and so forth. Without the proper support of society, it becomes difficult for the monks to survive in whatever situation they are in. There is an interdependency between the existence of monkhood and normal society in general. For the support system created by society for the monks, the monks have been returning the favor by providing service back to society. There is a barter based on this understanding between the monks and society. The monk is trained to provide help back to society without any expectation of any return. The service monks give back to society is not necessarily physical in nature. Monks share the knowledge gained from learning with teachers or through practice, which helps society walk on the right path and experience higher mental states. While some monks do provide help in the form of physical help, monks have been planting trees, digging ponds for water reserves, nursing the old and the sick, and many more. Monks also provide a reliable option for society to rely on in times of stress and fear. This creates a strong interdependency between the monks and society. In all these interactions between the monks and society, the monk is trained to help oneself as well as society without any expectation of money, recognition, or any sort of reciprocation.

The practice of service needs to be understood in its true essence and should also be translated into the everyday life of the individual living in society. Humans, as discussed earlier, are social animals. It becomes the sole responsibility of the individual to take care of the society one lives in without expectation of any return. This has to be the natural tendency of one's character to make lives easier for oneself as well as for the people around. The actions of service create a synchronized space of understanding between individuals, thus forging a strong bond of care and empathy. The synchronized space, which has resulted in forging the emotions of care and empathy, creates a feeling of love and friendship between the individuals living in society. Not only taking care of human beings that surround the individual but also rendering help and assistance to animals and the entirety of nature also falls under the category of undertaking the practice of service. Humans are not only dependent on other human beings but are also largely dependent on nature in its entirety. Human existence is most developed physically as well as mentally in comparison to other beings existing in the world. The responsibility has to be taken up by each and every individual to take care of nature, as the superiority of human existence lies in its attitude of taking care of and protecting the entirety of nature. The animal and plant kingdoms cannot voice expressively and clearly their wants and needs. The responsibility has to be taken up by human existence to serve nature as a whole. The individual must serve nature as a mark of gratitude rather than with the thought of doing some favor in reciprocation. For human society to exist without the support of nature, it is impossible. Each and every ecosystem in nature is responsible for nurturing human life. With this awareness, the individual must serve nature without any expectation of return, as nature has done its duty, is still doing it in the present, and will be doing it in the future too. The most important part of the support provided by nature is that it does not ask for any receipt in return. There is a selfless flow in the actions of nature, but with the presence of the conditioned mind in human existence, one cannot observe the selflessness one is surrounded by. It would be impossible to live without the sun rising and setting at its proper time, the rivers flowing in their intended directions, the flight of the birds, the flowering of trees and plants, the earth supporting and bearing all life forms, the flow of wind, and many more actions of nature. All these duties performed by nature are essential for all sorts of ecosystems to thrive, yet their actions are selfless. There is no expectation of any return or recognition hidden behind this flow of actions. The intentions behind these actions must be understood and implemented in one's own lifestyle and way of thinking. The intention is that it is one's own duty to evolve into the virtuous state of mind as well as take care of, protect, and facilitate the movement of all life forms, whether living or non-living, without any condition of return or recognition. Every individual has the duty of taking care of other human beings as well as all the facets of nature. According to one's own physical and mental capacity, the individual must help in serving humanity by providing them with the basic necessities of food, clothing, and shelter. At the same time, also maintain the balance of nature by planting trees, maintaining clean and pure water flow in the rivers, and reducing any contamination of any sort. Usually, in society, it is seen that acts of service are linked with the gaining of merits and demerits. With this thought process, the individual again gets entangled in the conditioned mind, where there is some condition of expectation. The expectation of gaining some merit in the future again becomes the cause of sorrow and delusion. This thought pattern must be shunned, and service to any life form must be seen as one's duty rather than as a source of buying merits for one's own self and recognition of any form in society. The actions in view of service are mentioned in short, and every individual, according to one's own circumstances, may find any suitable sort of service and follow it.

There is another aspect that service brings into an individual's life. The only pre-requisite for that aspect is to build awareness about these actions. In the duties of self-affirmations, the individual is used to certain expectations or reciprocation for some actions. The individual becomes habituated to the conditioned world while performing duties. The practice of service helps the individual decondition from the usual habit patterns of the mind while undertaking the duties of self-affirmation. Just as a monk is trained to perform all actions without expectation of any return, the individual must be trained to do so in order to have a better perspective on the duties of self-affirmations. In a practical sense, the individual must choose some duties in the world where the aim of the duty is not to fulfill one's own aspirations but to understand the significance of selfless service. In the previous chapter, the example of the mango tree was explained, where the fruition of mangoes on the tree is fulfillment of the mango seed's own aim of being in existence in the world. But the mango tree also facilitates a bunch of ecosystems around itself; this is the selfless service that the mango tree is providing to nature. Similarly, the individual must undertake some duties with the sole aim of only providing for society or nature in general, as it is becoming a part of humanity present in the individual.

For example, if an individual takes up the duty of sweeping a road or lane in a monastery or the society one lives in, and if this duty does not fall under the usual duties of self-affirmation, then the individual is surely going to find the practice of service difficult. When the individual encounters difficulty, the conditioned mind advises the individual to leave the duty midway and to resort to the usual habit patterns. But the individual walking on the path of the monk— mind—understands the true essence of undertaking the practice of service. The practice of service is to break the usual habit patterns of undertaking only the duties of self-affirmations. There is a certain level of ease behind undertaking these duties. The calibration of ease and habits of only undertaking the trained duties of the conditioned mind need to be broken. The individual starts sweeping the road or lane with a new understanding. The understanding that the individual does not have the proficiency of sweeping as it is not the usual habit pattern of the individual, but the intention of the individual must be such that each and every stroke in the action of sweeping must be undertaken to one's best of abilities. The best of one's abilities might not match up to the standards of professional sweepers, but the individual must accept that during the period of sweeping, one is just a mere sweeper, and it is the duty of oneself to make that lane or surrounding area as clean as possible and be open to crises and criticism of any sort. While, during the practice of service, the individual slowly develops the virtue of non-attachment, as true service does not entail any attachment to expectations. With the practice of service, the individual develops the immunity to undertake and withstand difficult duties in life. Not all actions in everyday life have to yield desired results, and the expectation of the desired result becomes a cause for sorrow and anger. As the individual's awareness deepens into the practice of service, they are able to withstand the absence of the desired result. With the absence of the desired result, the individual starts neglecting the duties of self-affirmations, and the practice of service in daily life ensures that, with or without the desired result of one's actions, the individual has to undertake these duties to the best of one's abilities. This practice helps in overriding the habit patterns of the conditioned mind with the natural state of mind, or the monk-mind. As the mango bearing on the mango tree, even with the right conditions, depends on the karmic conditionings of the mango seed, the fruition of human consciousness too depends on the karmic conditionings of the individual. It is important to remember that even if the mango tree is laden with fruit or not, it still serves a purpose of benefiting nature. It still helps in a lot of duties, such as maintaining the natural balance of the ecosystem. Similarly, like the mango tree, the development of human consciousness totally depends on the karmic conditions of the human being, but that does not stop the individual from putting in effort on that path. At the same time, even if the flowering of the human consciousness takes place or not, it is not of major consequence, but the existence of the individual for the purpose of facilitating life in society and in nature as a whole, without any conditions, must be understood and practiced. This understanding should create a space for the final fruition of the human consciousness according to one's ability to understand and be aware of it in the near future or present.

Monks in the monastery take care of the elder monks as a mark of gratitude and respect. The gratitude and respect are not enforced but come from the true nature of empathy, care, and selflessness for the service provided by the elders during their time of exuberance. The important point to be aware of is that even though service may seem like a wider aspect of individual existence, one should remember that, in a practical sense, true service starts at home or in relation to loved ones or people close by. The individual must not lose focus on the people they are surrounded by. Taking care of loved ones, especially the elderly, must become a priority in the space of existence of the individual. It is through the synchronized efforts of the people around one that one finds true solace. These efforts of the people one is surrounded by must not be forgotten, and a constant feeling of gratitude must be shown selflessly through the practice of service. The discussion about service may end up fruitless if the individual loses focus on the people nearby and wanders around in a totally opposite direction.

Prayer

Monks in monasteries or those who live alone usually have the habit of praying according to their respective lineage or faith. Prayer plays an important part in monk life. In monasteries, there is a fixed time for all the monks to unite and pray according to their lineage and faith. This system of praying together ensures that arrogance in monkhood does not seep in, and it also provides an act of remembrance of the values for which the individual has embraced monkhood. Prayer acts as a refresher for the monk to ponder the values and habit patterns that need to be followed. Rather than making prayer just a ritualistic part of their daily routine, a true monk looks upon the practice of prayer as an opportunity to ponder and reflect on the values laid down by the elders and teachers according to tradition or faith.

Secondly, there is an aspect of gratitude to the elders, teachers, or deities, if any. Monks are made to remember the sacrifice and effort put in by the elders so as to be aware of the values of tradition. The practice of prayer helps in maintaining a simple mindset at all times, for it helps in the development of the emotions of gratitude and thankfulness. The monk is reminded of the values and sacrifices the elders have gone through, and the monk in the present-day should look up to them and make an effort to emulate them in the present situation. As the evolution of the conditioned mind into the monk-mind is a continuous process, even monks can get affected by the effects of the conditioned mind, but with the practice of prayer in daily life, the monk is able to purify the intentions behind each and every action. It is very essential for the monk to have pure intentions behind each and every action. With pure intentions, the quality of monkhood of the individual increases rapidly, and the monk is able to live a guilt-free monk life for a long period of time. Essentially, prayer acts as a layer of protection for the life of the monk.

Just as a monk who practices praying as a daily life habit, the individual too can translate the habit into one's everyday life. The true aim of prayer needs to be understood, and a certain degree of awareness must be brought in while practicing it, rather than just making it a ritualistic endeavor. As discussed earlier, not all variables in existence are under individual control. But to understand and withstand the variables outside the bounds of individual effort, prayer plays an important role in surrendering the individual's existence in totality to those factors. That is why prayer is usually understood as total surrender. Total surrender to the factors of life that are not in individual control. The factors that are not in individual control are the effects of karmic conditioning and the movement of time and space. Prayer helps the individual to be aware of these factors and to understand the reality of these factors. With prayer, the individual is able to identify these factors and not get arrogant with the actions put in by self-effort. Just as a monk remembers the wholesome actions of the elders and teachers to remind oneself of the values and sacrifices expected from the present-day monk, the individual must use prayer as a tool to build up a mentality that can accept the variables that are not in individual control and surrender to those factors. The surrender happens through remembrance and gratitude toward the wholesome actions and sacrifices of teachers, elders, and the deity the individual believes in or feels connected to. The intention is to translate the wholesome qualities of the elders, teachers, and deities one believes in into one's own being. The transfer of those qualities can surely happen when there is gratitude, thankfulness, and surrender to the values, sacrifices, and actions of the past and present teachers, elders, and deities.

Does the practice of prayer come down to praying only to God or some higher being or deity? It is, of course, a beautiful practice to pray to God. It is important to surrender to some higher form of existence. One believes in a belief system depending on individual karmic conditionings. The intention is important here, not the object of worship or surrender. The intention is to translate the values of the object being worshipped. If someone finds it difficult to believe in the aforementioned concepts of God, teachers, and deities, there is still a way to pray according to the path of the monk's mind. One should remember that the practice of prayer is to manifest and facilitate the natural state of mind that the individual is already endowed with. That is why prayer should be a natural surrender of oneself rather than a fabricated one. Prayer can be a monotonous ritualistic endeavor without the proper understanding of the intention behind each and every action related to it. With proper intention, any individual walking the path of the monk—mind— can choose or affiliate with any object or identity as a figure for prayer and worship. There needs to be a natural connection. Individuals who have developed awareness can observe that they are surrounded by objects of reverence to pray to at all times. The practice of prayer is discussed ahead, and there is full freedom to adopt these practices as they need to come about naturally rather than being forced upon. It becomes easy for an individual who believes in praying to God, which is obviously revered and respected, but the discussion here is to find a common ground for each and every individual to pray in a simple manner with ease.

Prayer for the Monk: Mind

The individual on the path of the monk – mind is aware of all the objects to be inspired by at all times. The biggest motivating factor without which one cannot live is nature. The individual relies on nature for inspiration and values to depend upon. It is based on reality rather than any mythical descriptions. As one is always surrounded by some form of nature, it can act as a reminder for the individual to be grateful and thankful for. This prevents the individual from being arrogant, as there is always an aspect of nature to look up to rather than the conditioned habit of the individual to look down upon.

Prayer to Earth

It is an obvious fact that Earth is the basis of all types of creation in existence. The individual who wishes to develop higher mental states is aware of this fact. There is a deep sense of gratitude to the earthly element of nature. As it provides a strong foundation for life to sustain and provide nutrition. Just as a small baby relies on the mother for food and nutrition, the earth acts as a mother for all of creation by providing a base for nutrition and a foundation for living. Just like a mother, the earth has the quality and value of fortitude or endurance in it. The mother endures the pain of carrying a baby inside her womb for nine months and still does not complain and is even more grateful for the motherhood that the baby has granted her. Earth endures the weight of all living and non-living beings, as well as their material and physical aspirations. It does not ask for anything in return. The individual who is aware of these qualities will automatically bow down to the beauty of the qualities and values of the earth element and be grateful for being able to sustain life on it. The gratefulness will be with the intention that the immense fortitude and endurance that the earth element possesses be translated into one's own life so that it becomes effortless to walk on the path of the monk's mind. One should pray for the nourishing nature of the earth element to be translated into one's habit patterns and character, where one is able to nourish one's own body, breath, and mind, as well as the nature of relationships with all of existence.

The individual can be aware of all the qualities of nature around them, and with these qualities in mind, the individual can pray that these qualities become an inseparable part of life and behavior. For example, there could be awareness of the sun, moon, water, air, space, and the elements of nature in general. One could pray for the qualities of the sun to be translated into one. The quality of regularity that the sun depicts, the energy on which the entire universe depends, the soothing quality of the moon, the quality of water to cool down, the vastness of space to accept the entirety of existence—all these values and qualities could be prayed for by the individual to translate into habit patterns to uplift the mental state. Keeping in mind the values and qualities, the individual can pray to all aspects of nature, be it plants, trees, the mountains, rivers, etcetera. The individual, according to their experiences, has a sense of gratitude toward their parents, guardians, and loved ones who they think have influenced their way of life in a positive way. It could be a teacher or a stranger who, by coincidence, might have shaped the being of the individual.

What to pray for?

It does not matter to whom the individual prays, as it is a personal matter and depends upon the karmic conditionings of the individual. What really matters is: What does the individual pray for? Prayer is not meant for personal and material benefits, as all these benefits are not going to remain with the individual for long. The factor that the individual is going to be left with is their level of mental state. The individual must use the practice of prayer to achieve higher mental states by surrendering with awareness to the qualities and virtues of the object the individual is praying to. For enduring on the path of the monk-mind, it is very important to maintain a healthy body, as without a healthy body, it becomes very difficult for the individual to focus on the path of the monk-mind. With this awareness, the individual needs to pray that they develop a healthy and disease-free body. With a disease-free body, the individual must have a soothing breath flow in the body to improve concentration and mental peace. The individual should pray to have a soothing breath by which the body and the mind remain in synchronization. Without proper associations, it would be impossible for the individual to maintain steady growth on the path of the monk-mind. The individual must pray for constant association with the right company. The individual must pray for the total fruition of virtues in the mental state and experience a higher state of bliss, knowledge, and happiness, which gives the right view on how to live life according to the natural state of mind.

It is important to address the fact that all the living and non-living beings in the universe are connected through some sort of mentality without the barriers of region, state, religion, color, and sex. To walk the path of the monk—mind—is not only to pray for the fruition of only the individual's own state of being but for the entirety of existence as well. It is very important for the individual who wishes to understand and walk the monk-mind path to pray for the collective good of the entirety of existence. The entirety of existence must be in synchronization of understanding and peace, be it in the living or non-living realms, without any barriers, just to grow in love, understanding, health, and prosperity.

Friendship

The monks in the monasteries are trained to be simple. Simplicity is developed with the emotion of friendship. The monk is trained to view everyone in existence as a friend. Friendship is a form of intention, not outward behavior. Respect according to age differences and knowledge bases has to be respected; there is no questioning that. The monk is taught to keep away from judgments and have an open view toward treating everyone equally. The open view is that each and every individual in existence at every stage of being has some beauty aligned to it, and that beauty needs to be respected and adored rather than go under the scrutiny of any judgment. To be free and have acceptance of all beings in their way of being is taught to the monks so that they are protected from any arrogance or complexes from creeping in.

Of all the relationships in the world, the relationship of friendship is the most beautiful. To have a friend by one's side or to be a true friend to someone is the biggest of strengths one can be proud of. In the relationship of friendship, there is no expectation of any return, as there is only a sense of empathy and care that the individuals sharing that bond share. It creates a safe space for individuals to be themselves naturally, without any conditions. There is no judgment in the relationship of friendship. The judgment is based on any condition of the mind. The true values on which friendship is based are truth and honesty. Being truthful to the emotions that arise in the relationship and honest in their acceptance. On the basis of these two values, there comes a cessation of judgment and a view of total acceptance for one another.

Relationships according to the norms of society need to be followed, but the basis of all relationships should be the intention or emotion of friendship, and the basis of friendship should be truthfulness and honesty. When all these factors form the basis of one's interactions with oneself as well as with others, simplicity in one's own being naturally arises. On the basis of these values, there are no hidden agendas, selfishness, or deceit. There is clarity about one's actions and the relation of those actions to the other. One is able to see the reflection of oneself in others, which gives rise to a true form of empathy. The divisions based on hierarchy get dissolved, and total appreciation of each other's existence rises. With the evolution of the quality of friendship, the virtues of love and non-attachment have become perfect.

This is the reason that the relationship of friendship needs to be the basis of all relationships, be it the relationship with the parents, the spouse, with colleagues at work, or with teachers too. The relationship of a disciple with the guru is evidently one of friendship. There is, of course, an abundance of respect and love for the guru and vice versa, but it all stems from the basis of friendship and the aim to be simple in all aspects of life.

The simplicity of the mind is the main factor in achieving the monk-mind. Simplicity is best understood and flowered into character by the virtue of friendship. The virtue or emotion of friendship levels the plateaus of vices in the realm of human understanding. This is the natural state of the mind. There are certain religions in the East that have compared the emotion and relationship of friendship to God.

The Way Forward

The path of the monk - mind is to always move ahead without getting stuck on previous actions and happenings. It is to grow in understanding of virtues and continue the ascent on the path of higher mental states of existence. The path of the monk – mind does not guarantee any miracles. The greatest miracle an individual can experience is being born to experience the universe and its workings. It is to be free from the dream of any miracle or mysticism and to embrace the beauty of living in the present reality. The path of the monk—the mind—is not medicine for mental and physical ailments. It does not guarantee any remedies for such problems and ailments. The monk's mind is the total way of being for human existence. The way of existence is to develop immunity, both physically and mentally, to tackle and understand the objects and impressions of existence in the human mind. It provides a wholesome way to live life with the qualities of empathy, love, and understanding. The understanding is not intended to be imparted to the individual but also to the entirety of society as a whole.

The path of the monk-mind is the unification of knowledge and action. Action, which takes place on the basis of knowledge, which has risen from wisdom, and wisdom, which has risen from the understanding of virtues, The path of evolving knowledge is based on the practice of awareness of intention; awareness of intention gives rise to wisdom, and wisdom gives rise to the development of knowledge. Knowledge is the know-how of the way an individual must undertake actions in his or her existence. This foolproof way of life is being tried to be achieved by the working of the monk – mind. The way of self-belief and confidence is the way of the monk- mind. The confidence and self-belief, which have not risen from arrogance but from the development of the understanding of virtues and wisdom in character and understanding, there is total acceptance of the natural law of existence, which is of constant change and impermanence. Understanding this natural law and translating it into character and understanding is true wisdom and knowledge. The monk-mind makes it easy for the individual to accept and practice the wisdom with ease and intensity.

The light of wisdom that lightens in the human realm makes way for true and complete freedom. All the questions and doubts that arise begin to wane. The individual becomes truly independent in one's own way of life. There arises intuitive knowledge, which has the power to quell all doubts and questions. One is able to observe the rise of the guru and guide in oneself. The light of wisdom is the guru and the master, which are present in each and every individual. This light of guidance subsequently guides the individual by removing the darkness of the habit patterns of the conditioned mind. The light of the self helps in identifying one's own individual path and provides the necessary energy to walk on the chosen path. It has to be remembered regularly that the path has to be walked rather than just questioning or thinking about it. Whatever the individual path one may choose, the books aim at providing the final push to jump on the desired path with true intentions. Once the jump has been made, the path of the individual takes care of itself, provided the individual has the right intention, total faith, and surrenders to the teachings of their respective paths.

This book is a gift from all the teachers and monks the author has been in contact with, be it physically or subtly. The content that makes sense to the reader must be seen as the grace and gift of all the teachers and monks to whom the author is grateful. The content, which the reader does not subscribe to, may be seen as a foolish endeavor by the author, and the reader may go ahead and forgive the author for his petty shenanigans. I am praying for peace in existence for everyone to grow in love, patience, and courage with higher and more beautiful mental states.

About the Author

Mytri Sanatkumar is a monk who has had the fortune of practicing and understanding spiritual texts and practices under the traditions of the Sanatana Dharma in India (Bharat) and the Buddhist practices in Sri Lanka. He was initiated at a young age into the practices of Pranayama and meditation by his spiritual master Sri Tathata. Since then, he has had the guidance and direction in practices, rituals and philosophies from Sri Tathata at various points of time. After completing his university education, Mytri under the guidance of his master was sent to learn under different teachers and gurus in India (Bharat). The search for learning and understanding different spiritual texts and practices have led Mytri to undergo training at different monasteries in Bharat. Some of the notable places being the holy city of Varanasi, Sringeri and the famous Panini Mahavidyalaya in Sonipat Haryana. While learning in these holy places Mytri has had the opportunity to learn from many notable teachers and monks who belong to the Sanatana Dharma tradition, and was able to learn the Sanskrit grammar and many other spiritual texts and practices. Of the practices which he learnt he wishes to continue, is the fire practice according to Vedic tradition with daily meditations and Yoga practice. While learning and practicing under these teachers and gurus he had the constant guidance and support of his master Sri Tathata. After the period of learning and practicing in Bharat he was guided by Sri Tathata to understand the path of the Buddha. This direction led him to join the forest monastery belonging to the Theravada tradition of Buddhism in Sri Lanka. In The holy land of Sri Lanka, he was initiated into the Buddhist Monk order as a Samanera. His initiated name into Buddhism is India Mettavasa. During his time learning and practicing in Sri Lanka he had newer insights into the path of meditation and wisdom according to the Buddhist teachings. With the aim of uniting the path of the Buddha and the teachings of the rishis and provide a common ground of spirituality irrespective of caste, gender and societal status Mytri is continuing his practice with Sri Tathata.

Mytri is a graduate in Electrical and Electronics Engineering and a Yoga teacher. He is an avid sports and music lover and shares a love for the game of football and Hindustani classical music.

You can contact Myri for queries and discussions at the given email address.

mytrisanatkumar07@gmail.com

themonkmindforyou@gmail.com

www.ingramcontent.com/pod-product-compliance
Lightning Source LLC
Chambersburg PA
CBHW051147130726

47988CB00005B/2029